Yes, You Can Forgive! But Do You Want To?

Hans E. Ngodock

Copyright © 2024 Hans E. Ngodock
All rights reserved.
ISBN: 9798337716244

DEDICATION

To my dear mother, the late Nkottè Wanga Ruth, in whose life I observed love and forgiveness, and to my wife, Berthe (Princesse), and our four children, Giovanni, Mo, Pep and Ruthie (as I affectionately call them), with whom I learned and am still learning to practice love and forgiveness on a daily basis.

CONTENTS

	Foreword	i
	Introduction	1
1	Handling Offenses	2
2	Offenses, Offenses, and More Offenses	5
3	Examples Galore	7
4	Unforgiveness	9
5	Spiritualizing Unforgiveness	13
6	The Ratio of Debts	17
7	Unforgiveness Will Make a Murderer Out of You	19
8	The Case of Esau and Jacob	26
9	God's Perspective	29
10	Wounds of the Heart	31
11	You Cannot Forgive from a Wounded Heart	33
12	Lack of Understanding	35
13	Forgiveness and Love	40
14	God's Love	42
15	Do I Have this Love?	46
16	In His Presence	50
17	Some Examples in the Bible	54
18	Personal Stories	57
19	Back to Love	60
20	A Heart of Forgiveness	62
21	Partakers of the Divine Nature	70
22	My Mother's House	73
23	Ignorance Much?	77
24	From the Mission Field	87
25	Provision for Ignorance	93
26	Stark Warnings	97
27	Last But Not Least	100
	References	103
	About the Author	104

FOREWORD

Hans has written a wonderful book packed with practical application on forgiveness. Drawing lessons from his own life and lacing it with Biblical truth, he points the way through the swamp of unforgiveness. Often, followers of Jesus lose their way on the journey because of offenses that are never dealt with or processed properly. The enemy of your soul has devised a snare to keep you from reaching spiritual maturity, and he baits the trap with hurt and bitterness. This book will serve as a guide from "being wounded" to living in "authentic forgiveness."

The author engages the reader with real life examples and personal stories that will give the reader insight into his personal struggle to find healing and forgiveness. Also, he teaches the truth of this pressing topic through the lives and stories of Biblical characters. Hans has a unique ability to draw out hidden principles embedded in the stories and then show us real life applications on how to get free and remain that way.

I highly recommend this book for your personal development as well as a study guide on forgiveness for small groups. It will also serve as a resource for pastors preparing a sermon on this topic.

--Doug McAllister

Senior Pastor of Journey Fellowship Church, Slidell, Louisiana

INTRODUCTION

There is a reason why you picked this book to read. You may have been attracted by the title, or someone may have told you about it. I don't believe in randomness when it comes to the things of God; He always has a purpose. Many books have already been written on the topic of forgiveness–from different perspectives, from clinical psychology to religion. I am not a clinician or a psychologist. And though I am a pastor and missionary, I did not set out to write this book from that standpoint. Because offenses and the unforgiveness they generate in our hearts vary by their nature and the pain they inflict, it is difficult to even imagine that there could be a common solution to everyone's unforgiveness problems.

In this book, I am taking you on my personal journey of offenses and forgiveness, hoping that what I have learned so far can be helpful for your case as well. You will notice that I do not cite any other book except the Bible. This is intentional, as I want you, the reader, to anchor your understanding of this sensitive and dangerous issue not on the wisdom of men, but on the word of God, just as I did. There may be some aspects of the problem that I will not deal with in this book. I only hope that, as I write from what is flowing from my heart, the areas that I touch will be sufficient to convey what I believe God wanted you to get from reading this book. All the Bible quotations in this book are taken from the New King James Version (NKJV) and are within the "Gratis Use Guidelines."

1 HANDLING OFFENSES

Consider the interaction between Jesus and Peter at Caesarea Philippi. After Peter receives the revelation from God the Father and confesses that Jesus is the Christ, the Son of the living God, Jesus commands the disciples not to tell anyone that He is the Christ. He also began to tell them how He was going to suffer many things in Jerusalem and eventually be killed.

In Matthew 16:22, we read that, "Peter took Him aside and began to rebuke Him …" In verse 23, we read that Jesus turned and said to Peter, "Get behind Me, Satan! You are an offense to Me, …" A slightly different rendition is given in Mark 8:33 that says, "But when He had turned around and looked at His disciples, He rebuked Peter, saying, "Get behind Me, Satan!" It is clear to me that Jesus took Peter's rebuke as an offense, yet, we must pay close attention to how He handled the offense. His reply to Peter was in the form of a rebuke. I have always wondered how any person, including myself, would react to such rebuke. Jesus is looking at Peter, speaking to him (Matthew's version) and rebuking him (Mark's version) with the words, "Get behind me, Satan!" But Jesus obviously was not calling Peter Satan, since He had just called him Petros in the preceding verses. And it seems to me that Peter was not offended at the rebuke either, because he must have understood and discerned that Jesus's words, as harsh as they were, were meant to pull him out of the wrong mindset of letting his emotions dictate his relationship with Jesus, an enemy's trap into which we fall way too easily and too often.

Although Peter's rebuke was an offense to Jesus, we don't see Him reacting as an angry and offended person. Likewise, we don't see Peter getting offended at Jesus's rebuke, because he did not take it personally. Many of us would be offended for much less of an insult, not to mention being called or associated with Satan, at least on the surface. May God help us to handle offensive situations properly.

We tend to perceive and process offenses as a devaluation and rejection of our worth, of who we are at the core. We see them as the manifestation of hatred, the lack of love. Furthermore, our natural reaction to offenses is to show an equal or greater amount of rejection and lack of love to the offender. Since we will be dealing with offenses at a personal level, it is good for us to realize from the outset that at times, Jesus was also offended on a personal level. Consider the Pharisees' attitude towards Jesus: they were always accusing Him of breaking God's Law and committing blasphemy, criticizing Him and even plotting to destroy Him. Jesus could also easily claim to have been offended by the Pharisees. Yet, we see Him accepting the invitation to dine with Simon, a Pharisee (Luke 7:36-50), and engaging in a friendly conversation about salvation with Nicodemus (John 3), a Pharisee and ruler of the Jews. Contrast that with the Pharisees who also felt offended by Jesus's teachings, but rather planned to destroy Him.

It is not only the Pharisees who took offense at some of Jesus's teachings. The disciples were offended at Jesus's words in John 6, and many stopped following Him. What a spiritual tragedy! The few who continued with Him understood that He had the *"words of eternal life,"* as Peter summarized in John 6:68. The same Peter was *"grieved"* (which can also be rendered as offended) in John 21:17 when Jesus asked him for the third time if he loved Him. It is not that Jesus intended to offend Peter. The conversation may have just reminded Peter of his three denials of Jesus after he had vehemently claimed to stand for and by Jesus, even if he had to die with Him. This rather emotional conversation did not drive Peter away from Jesus, nor did it keep Peter from serving Jesus to the end of his life. He valued eternal life and his relationship with Jesus more than the temporary inconvenience that Jesus's words, being the truth, could cause him at a personal level. We also need, like Peter, to look beyond the potential offense and focus on eternal life.

2 OFFENSES, OFFENSES, AND MORE OFFENSES

I was teaching a small group Bible study at my church a few years ago, and we came across the topic of forgiveness. I was surprised by two reactions from the small group members. One person flatly said, without hesitation or emotion, "I cannot forgive them for what they have done." Two years later, I was discussing this topic with pastors in Ouagadougou (Burkina Faso) during a mission trip. That's where I learned of a saying in the country that goes like this: "Even in heaven, I will not forgive you." What a statement! It is not only poignant; to me, such a statement reveals four things about forgiveness:

1. It is difficult to forgive.
2. There are misconceptions about the subject.
3. The person making the statement has a level of spiritual immaturity.
4. The person making this statement and believing it to be true is greatly deceived. Unforgiveness will not make it to heaven.

I am not writing just about other people's experiences. I was faced with the difficulty of forgiving an offense, and it took years and a revelation from God to overcome it (more on this later). As I gained some more insight and understanding on the subject and began sharing my experience, people around me started encouraging me to write.

I usually begin teaching this topic by asking the following questions: Who has never been offended? And who has never offended anyone? Of course, the answers to these questions are obvious. Everyone has been offended at least once, and everyone has, at least once in their lifetime, offended someone else. The next question I ask also has an obvious answer: Who loves and enjoys being forgiven? Everyone that I know. Jesus warned us that there would be offenses. He says in Luke 17:1, "It is impossible that no offenses should come ..." In other words, the opportunities to be offended will always be around. So, why is it so hard for people, including myself, to forgive? Offenses always seem to catch us by surprise, especially when they come from people from whom we least expect to be offended. Some offenses reach the depths of our emotions, either because of the gravity of the offense or the level of relationship we have with the offender.

It would be wrong for us to assume that offenses only come from unbelievers. Unfortunately, they also come from believers. Many people have walked away from churches because of offenses, and this is not just in today's times. The early disciples faced this problem too; otherwise, the apostle Paul would have had no reason to exhort the believers in churches to forgive one another (Ephesians 4:32, Colossians 3:13), a failure that resulted in the Corinthian believers taking each other to court (1 Corinthians 6:7).

Some offenses are legit, as when we are the direct target of an attack. Other offenses are tangential, as when we take offense for some wrong that was not directed at us, or when our ego feels slighted. Yet, other offenses are frivolous, such as the ones that are displayed every day in today's society for the sake of advancing a particular agenda.

3 EXAMPLES GALORE

As I write on this topic, I am returning from a mission trip. I sat down with a beloved brother who poured out his heart to me as he described the horrible pain and emotional trauma he was going through. He was happily married with two children. A marriage conflict was instigated by another brother, a pastor nonetheless, who encouraged the man's wife to leave the family home and lodge temporarily at his own pastor's home. As I write, this wife has not returned home to her husband and kids. To make matters worse, she is now pregnant by the brother of the pastor who temporarily lodged her. No wonder the brother said, "I don't know if I can forgive him." When he made this statement before providing the details of his situation, I was wondering why a brother who seemed to be well established in the faith would arrive at this conclusion. But after hearing his story, I wondered if I myself could forgive in this situation.

A gifted minister of the gospel, happily married with children, felt called to go start a ministry in another country. Life became difficult for him in the new country, so much so that instead of returning home like the prodigal son, he had to marry a citizen of this country in order to remain there legally and be able to work. Think about the wife and children he left in his country of origin. No amount of financial support will ever erase or heal the pain of such betrayal. How can they forgive?

A friend of mine founded a church and toiled to pastor it. He served in the church for decades, raising many sons and daughters in ministry at various levels. When the Lord called him home, he left behind the church, a widow, children, and grandchildren. In the months that preceded his going to be with the Lord, while he was battling sickness in the hospital, he had appointed someone to preach in his place. Eventually, this person became the new pastor. During and after all the preparations for the funeral, the church did not contribute a single cent. Keep in mind that my friend is the one who trained and appointed even the person serving as the church administrator at the time of his death. Now, his widow is not even consulted for any matter regarding the operation of the church. For a long time, every conversation I had with her was tainted with bitterness at the mention of these events. In fact, most conversations would end up revolving around the story of the hurts, even though she had told the story many times. You could tell the heart was still hurt and the wound was still open, thus, forgiveness had not yet taken place.

You probably have your own case or cases of offenses that are equally painful, or even worse. Maybe you are one of the people who are the victims of rape, trapped in human and sex trafficking, children abandoned by parents, who have been abused by people in positions of trust, sometimes even within the family, or the victims of many other evils.

4 UNFORGIVENESS

Unforgiveness is the essence of holding on to the hurts and offenses we have suffered and wishing and harboring the desire of revenge on the perpetrators. And when we cannot exact revenge, we just wish evil on them.

Unforgiveness is wickedness! In a parable that Jesus Himself taught in Matthew 18:32, a master says to an unforgiving servant, "You wicked servant! I forgave you all that debt because you begged me."

Unforgiveness is also a double destroyer: the person holding onto unforgiveness is feeling the pain of the offense while also suffering from all of its negative emotional, physical, and psychological effects. Of course, there are also spiritual effects and consequences, because Jesus taught us that if we do not forgive, the Father in heaven will not forgive us, either. So, it appears that when God commands us to forgive, He is actually trying to spare us all of the destruction that unforgiveness brings. I wish the destruction of unforgiveness could remain contained to the unforgiving offended person. That is not the case, unfortunately. See, unforgiveness negatively impacts everything that the offended person does or is emotionally connected to, and for those involved in ministry, this includes their ministry as well, with all its ramifications.

Let's look at a few examples of unforgiveness in the Bible:

1. The prophet Elisha cursed the youth who were mocking him (2 Kings 2:23–24). You may rightfully wonder what that has to do with unforgiveness. My simple observation is that the prophet could have ignored the mocking youths, or he could have forgiven them in his heart and moved on, but he took the offense, instead. I am not condoning or justifying the youth's irreverent and disrespectful behavior; I am deliberately only highlighting the lack of forgiveness in this case.

2. The sons of Zebedee ask for fire to come down on a Samaritan village that did not welcome Jesus (Luke 9:51–56). Rightfully, Jesus rebukes them by reminding them that "the Son of Man did not come to destroy men's lives, but to save them." This is exactly the principle that is at play in Elisha's case with the mocking youths.

3. My favorite example is Jonah. We are all familiar with the story of Jonah. If not, you can read the whole story in the Bible (Book of Jonah), which consists of only four short chapters. Notice that we are talking here about a seasoned servant of God, one who is able to clearly hear from God and speak to the people on God's behalf. Jonah hears God telling him to go speak to the people of Nineveh. He refuses to go there and heads to Tarshish, instead, which is basically the opposite way. He will suffer the consequences of his disobedience by spending three days and three nights inside the belly of a great fish. Before you dismiss this story as fictional, just remember that Jesus himself reminded his audience about the story of Jonah.

Anyway, after the great fish spits out Jonah at God's command, he reluctantly goes to Nineveh and delivers a doom-filled message. Talk about wishing ill to someone! To his surprise, the people of Nineveh repent and turn to God, who forgives them. This outcome makes the prophet so angry that he asks God to take his life. Jonah would rather die than see God forgive an entire city. Think about it: a servant of God did not rejoice at the fact that God forgave a repenting city. What was it again that Jesus said about one sinner who repents? That's right, joy in heaven! But not to Jonah. I venture here to say that all of this is rooted in Jonah's unforgiveness towards Nineveh.

History tells us about the brutality, violence, and cruelty that the Assyrians inflicted on the peoples they defeated in their glory days, and Jonah took offense at the evils and wickedness of the people of Nineveh. At the time of Jonah, the Assyrians had not yet attacked or invaded Israel. So, Jonah is taking offense at wrongs he did not suffer. Not that he should not empathize with the victims of the Assyrian violence. But here we see that anger, resentment, bitterness, and, of course, unforgiveness towards the Ninevites have clouded and blinded Jonah's judgment to the point that he is willing to disobey God and suffer the consequences rather than obey. It is not far-fetched to conclude this, because Jonah himself tells God that he knew God would show mercy to the Ninevites, and that is why he did not want to obey the command to go there. In other words, Jonah did not want them to be forgiven. Unfortunately, this is a sad manifestation of unforgiveness. We don't want the offender to be forgiven or to be blessed; rather, we wish all sorts of evil would befall them.

I want to remind you that God loves everyone equally. He loves your offenders just as much as He loves you. See, unforgiveness is a bait from the enemy. It takes us to the place where we decide who deserves to be forgiven and who does not, a prerogative that belongs to God alone. In other words, unforgiveness will lure you to take the place of God, the very thing that the enemy tried to do but failed and was cast out of heaven. Now, the same enemy tricks people with unforgiveness so that they end up in the camp of those ejected from heaven.

Unforgiveness is therefore more harmful than the offenses we suffered in the first place, because the enemy hides behind unforgiveness to lure and lead you into perdition. Don't take the bait, however justifiable your unforgiveness is, whatever level of wrong you have suffered and pain you are going through. The further tragedy of the story of Jonah and Nineveh is that Jonah was so consumed by anger and unforgiveness towards the Ninevites that he chose not to be part of the great revival that was taking place. Why is this a ministry tragedy? Imagine hundreds of thousands of people turning to the Lord with no mature believer available to disciple them. No wonder Nineveh fell back into sin and idolatry. That's a great ministry tragedy to me. May God help us to never reach that point where souls that could be saved are lost because of our unforgiveness.

5 SPIRITUALIZING UNFORGIVENESS

Some people hide their unforgiveness in spiritual prayers, even quoting the Bible verses that call for God's vengeance. Of course, I believe that God is the God of vengeance. But He is also the God of mercy. In fact, the Bible does not make vengeance part of God's character or attributes. Many times in the Scriptures, we read that "God is merciful" (Deuteronomy 4:31, 2 Chronicles 30:9, Psalms 59:5, Psalms 103:8, 116:5, 117:2, Jeremiah 3:12, Joel 2:13, James 5:11), but I have yet to read a single verse that says God is vengeful, even though God says that vengeance is His (Deuteronomy 32:35, Romans 12:19, Hebrews 10:30). Listen to how God introduces Himself in Exodus 34:6-7, "[6]And the Lord passed before him and proclaimed, 'The Lord, the Lord God, merciful and gracious, longsuffering, and abounding in goodness and truth, [7] keeping mercy for thousands, forgiving iniquity and transgression and sin, by no means clearing the guilty, visiting the iniquity of the fathers upon the children and the children's children to the third and the fourth generation.'" In other words, vengeance does not describe God; it is not part of His character or nature, as are mercy, grace, and longsuffering, i.e., patience. We all know by definition that mercy is when punishment is withheld from someone who deserves to be punished.

When someone has been hurt and offended and prays to God to avenge them, they are actually asking God to mete the vengeance that they themselves would have carried out. They still want to retaliate, but now they want God to do it for them. To me, this is an attempt to use God's power to satisfy a personal desire, a trick that the devil used in the wilderness when he asked Jesus to turn stones into bread. Just as Jesus resisted, we must also resist this temptation. Asking God to take revenge on our offenders on our behalf won't work, because God is more interested in mercy and forgiveness, both yours and the offender's, than in revenge and judgment. People actually go crazy about this because they usually see that God is not avenging them; instead, they see the offender faring well.

If you are hoping and waiting for God to avenge you on your offenders, you may be in for a long wait. Exodus 34:7 says that God will keep His mercy for a thousand generations. In Revelation 6:10, those who had been slain for the word of God and for the testimony which they held ask God: "How long, O Lord, holy and true, until You judge and avenge our blood on those who dwell on the earth?" These people are in heaven; some may have been martyred centuries or millennia ago, and God has still not yet avenged them. Instead, they are being asked to rest a little longer until the number of their fellow martyrs is completed. Translation: God has a plan; that plan includes offenses, and for some, the plan includes suffering martyrdom.

If God were to execute vengeance promptly upon the offenders, as our offended and hurt hearts often desire, Cain would not have lived another day after murdering his brother, Abel, nor would the people who condemned Jesus (God's own son), nor the apostle Paul for the murder of Stephen. Many other examples can be found in the Bible, and we may wonder why. It is not that God is not aware of their wickedness. God is more driven by mercy than by judgment. As the Bible says, "mercy triumphs over judgment" (James 2:13). This verse is supported by other verses. In Ezekiel 18:23, God Himself says through the prophet, "Do I have any pleasure at all that the wicked should die?" says the Lord God, "and not that he should turn from his ways and live?" We read something similar in Ezekiel 33:11. "Say to them: 'As I live,' says the Lord God, 'I have no pleasure in the death of the wicked, but that the wicked turn from his way and live. Turn, turn from your evil ways! For why should you die, O house of Israel?'"

In other words, God shows patience towards the wicked and desires that the wicked will repent and be forgiven. In Romans 2:4, the apostle Paul tells us, "Or do you despise the riches of His goodness, forbearance, and longsuffering, not knowing that the goodness of God leads you to repentance?" See, God's desire is that all men and women, all of them, and yes, that includes all of the offenders out there, both yours and mine, would repent, come to the knowledge of the truth in Christ Jesus, and be forgiven and saved, according to 1 Timothy 2:3–4: "³For this is good and acceptable in the sight of God our Savior, ⁴who desires all men to be saved and to come to the knowledge of the truth."

That's right! God desires to save and forgive all men and women, including your offenders.

The Shipwreck

Some other people go a little further by turning the anger that goes along with their unforgiveness towards God. They blame Him for what has happened. This is often the case of individuals who have been abused by someone who had civil or spiritual authority over them. Examples abound of people who would have nothing to do with God because they were offended by someone in or associated with the church. Just how many times have you, the reader, heard someone say that the church is filled with hypocrites? Chances are that people who make such declarations have been offended by the church in some way. These people actually ask the right question about why the offense has happened to them, but they don't linger in God's presence long enough to get the answers. Instead, they take the easy but costly and tragic way of turning their back on God. Not that God would immediately answer all their questions, but turning away from God is like refusing to take the only medication that would eventually cure a deadly disease or refusing to go to the only physician who could treat it.

Although they do not specifically fit this description, it is still safe to include Cain and Jonah in this category. We will discuss how Cain was offended from another perspective. He did not take his offense to God for healing. Quite the opposite happened to him, in that it was God who came to him. Cain still found a way to reject God's counsel and take matters into his own hands, basically turning away from God. The same can be said of Jonah. As discussed earlier, he was offended by the violence and cruelty of the people of Nineveh, and, instead of drawing closer to God through obedience, he decided to run away and hide from God, which is essentially turning away from God. There is no better illustration of turning away from God than willfully setting out to go in the opposite direction of where God is sending and to do what someone knows is contrary to God's will.

6 THE RATIO OF DEBTS

As He was teaching forgiveness, Jesus told the parable of two people owing money to creditors (Matthew 18:22–34). The first debtor owed 10,000 talents to his master. The story does not tell how a servant came to owe so much money. He realized he could never repay the debt, went to his master, and asked to be forgiven. Without hesitation, the master had mercy on him and forgave all the debt. This same servant turned around and found a fellow servant who owed him 100 denarii. This servant also pleaded for mercy and forgiveness because he could not pay the debt. Instead of forgiving just as he himself was forgiven, the first servant grabbed his fellow servant and began to beat him up, almost choking him. Notice in the story that the second servant used exactly the same words that the first servant had used, pleading for mercy. The second servant went a little further–he begged! You would assume that a person who has just had his debts (of the not-so-small amount of 10,000 talents) canceled out of mercy would understand and also have mercy enough to cancel a debt of 100 denarii that someone else owed him. The servant who owed the 100 denarii pleaded for mercy and begged to no avail.

A denarius was the daily wage for a day laborer, who typically worked 11 to 12 hours from 6 a.m. to 6 p.m. So, the second servant owed the equivalent of 100 days of work. They could possibly make an arrangement. A talent, on the other hand, is worth 6,000 denarii, so the first servant's debt was 600,000 times the debt of the one who owed him 100 denarii. As I said, it is hard to imagine how a servant came to owe that much money; it is even harder to imagine how he could pay it back, earning a servant's wages, possibly a denarius per day. You get the point: it was impossible for this servant to repay his master. He could not work hard enough or long enough, even if he were to live a few lifetimes.

Consider a Jewish lunar calendar of 28 days per month, with no work on Sabbath days. In a year, assuming no other breaks, a laborer would have worked 288 days. So, in the best-case scenario, it would take about 208 years of work to accumulate the 10,000 talents, assuming that all the wages are saved toward repaying the debt. However, this servant had a family to feed and probably other expenses, including taxes. Besides, who can possibly have the strength to be a day laborer for these many years? It was no longer the time of the Adams and Methuselahs and Noahs who lived hundreds of years being healthy; Caleb kept his youthful strength into his eighties (Joshua 14:10–11).

It is this servant who cannot pay back his debt, who acknowledges it and tells his creditor, who receives mercy and the cancellation of his debt, who turns around, grabs his fellow servant who owes him 100 denarii, and begins to beat him to death to get his money back, after the man has pleaded with him and begged for mercy, just as he himself had done earlier. As the story goes, some other servants who had witnessed the master forgiving the debt of 10,000 talents also saw this servant beating up his fellow servant over the 100 denarii debt, denying him mercy. They were grieved at his treatment of his debtor, so, they went and told it to the master, and the master summoned the man. As the man came to the master, the master called him "wicked."

7 UNFORGIVENESS WILL MAKE A MURDERER OUT OF YOU

You would think that the servant who wants to kill his fellow servant for 100 denarii is an isolated case. Unfortunately, it is not! We know from the story that his actions were motivated by unforgiveness.

A believer in Christ and faithful church member who was well-involved in the church discovered that his wife fell into adultery with another member of the same church. I remember having a conversation with the betrayed brother. At some point, he said, without hesitation, that he would kill the brother who committed adultery with his wife. At the time, I attributed his statement to anger and pain. Now, however, I understand his statement more in light of unforgiveness.

I was preaching last year at one of the churches in Sierra Leone on the life of Jacob and came to the part where he stole his brother's blessing. I paused for a few seconds, then asked the church the question in this manner: What would you do to a person who stole the blessing that you have been waiting for all your life? A lady actually exclaimed out loud that she would kill that person. Never mind that this was during a Sunday morning church service!

Let's also look at other examples in the Bible.

Cain and Abel (Genesis 4:1-8)

Cain is another example; he got offended at his brother Abel when his offering was not respected by God, who respected Abel's offering. Cain's initial reaction to God not respecting his offering is described in verse 5 as, "very angry, and his countenance fell." We are not told to whom his anger was directed, but we can safely assume it was towards his brother. He took offense at the fact that his brother's offering was respected, but his own was not. The offense was deep enough in his heart that he could not forgive his brother, but he decided to kill him. Notice that Abel actually had nothing to do with Cain's offering not being accepted by God. Abel did not tell Cain what to offer; he did not deceive his brother into offering something he knew God would not respect, so that only his offering would be accepted. Neither did he tell God which offering to accept. In other words, Abel did nothing offensive to Cain, at least not intentionally or directly. How do I know? God Himself asks Cain, "If you do well … will you not be accepted?" In other words, God's acceptance was conditional based on the actions, not the offerings themselves.

Our gracious God saw the offense growing in Cain's heart, and He took the initiative to come talk to Cain and counsel him. Unfortunately, not even a conversation with God could turn his anger away from his brother. In the end, he despised God's counsel, rose up, and killed him, because this was an offense that he could not forgive. What happened to Cain continues to happen today. We quite often take offense at people who did not offend us intentionally or directly. We must guard our hearts, though, and not let the offenses grow so deep that the voice and counsel of God Himself become meaningless to us. Can God speak to your offended heart? Will you follow whatever direction or advice He gives your offended heart?

King Saul

In 1 Samuel 18, we are told that after David had killed Goliath, the Philistine's giant, as King Saul's army was coming home, the Israelite women came out of all their cities to celebrate their army's victory. We read in verse 6, "Now it had happened as they were coming home, when David was returning from the slaughter of the Philistine, that the women had come out of all the cities of Israel, singing and dancing, to meet King Saul, with tambourines, with joy, and with musical instruments." Notice that the purpose of this gathering and celebration was to meet King Saul. However, their song in verse 7, "Saul has slain his thousands, and David his ten thousands," did not go over well with King Saul. In verse 9, we read, "Saul eyed David from that day forward." The term "eyed" used in this translation can also be translated as "viewed with suspicion," "viewed with hatred," or "viewed with envy." This is what we often do with our offenders: we view them with suspicion. It is obvious to me that King Saul got offended that the women ascribed greater honor of the battle victory to David than himself. From this offense, he set out to destroy David by all means possible.

I would like to draw your attention to the fact that David, who now comes first on King Saul's list of people to kill, did nothing offensive to Saul. There was no action from David that was directed at Saul, much less with offensive intent. David did not tell the women what to sing about. If anything, he delivered Saul from defeat and shame, and through that victory, he delivered the entire nation of Israel. I could probably understand if the anger coming from Saul's offended heart was directed at the women. After all, they are the ones who sang the song and danced, not David. But Saul took offense at David. The offense was so deep in Saul's heart that at some point, he insulted, cursed, and tried to kill his own son, Jonathan, who was trying to bring him back to reason (1 Samuel 20:32–33).

Saul was offended because of his own pride! Instead of celebrating the huge victory, regardless of who the hero was, his ego was hurt and took over his reason, resulting in an offended heart. If we do not keep our egos in check, we will likely fall into the same trap as Saul.

Ahab and Jezebel

The following story is taken from 1 Kings 21. The first seven verses set the context:

> "[1] And it came to pass after these things that Naboth the Jezreelite had a vineyard which was in Jezreel, next to the palace of Ahab, king of Samaria. [2] So Ahab spoke to Naboth, saying, 'Give me your vineyard, that I may have it for a vegetable garden, because it is near, next to my house; and for it I will give you a vineyard better than it. Or, if it seems good to you, I will give you its worth in money.' [3] But Naboth said to Ahab, 'The Lord forbid that I should give the inheritance of my fathers to you!' [4] So Ahab went into his house sullen and displeased because of the word which Naboth the Jezreelite had spoken to him; for he had said, 'I will not give you the inheritance of my fathers.' And he lay down on his bed, and turned away his face, and would eat no food. [5] But Jezebel his wife came to him, and said to him, 'Why is your spirit so sullen that you eat no food?' [6] He said to her, 'Because I spoke to Naboth the Jezreelite, and said to him, 'Give me your vineyard for money; or else, if it pleases you, I will give you another vineyard for it.' And he answered, 'I will not give you my vineyard.' [7] Then Jezebel his wife said to him, 'You now exercise authority over Israel! Arise, eat food, and let your heart be cheerful; I will give you the vineyard of Naboth the Jezreelite.' "

King Ahab was obviously offended by Naboth's refusal to sell to him (the king) the property that he (Naboth, a subject) had inherited from his ancestors. Naboth's stance was in obedience to

God's law, while King Ahab was seeking convenience. Much like Cain, Ahab's offended heart caused his spirit to become sullen, and eventually his countenance also fell, because his wife Jezebel could see that something was not right about him. After explaining the reason for his sadness to his wife, she conspired to have Naboth killed and to seize the coveted piece of land. Although the idea of killing Naboth did not originate from Ahab, he still consented and enjoyed the outcome of this sinister scheme. No wonder God himself would send the prophet Elijah to rebuke him with the words, "Have you murdered and also taken possession?" (verse 19).

Haman the Son of Hammedatha

In the third chapter of the book of Esther, we read of the promotion of Haman to become second in command to King Ahasuerus, who ruled an empire stretching from India to Ethiopia:

> "After these things, King Ahasuerus promoted Haman, the son of Hammedatha the Agagite, and advanced him and set his seat above all the princes who were with him. ² And all the king's servants who were within the king's gate bowed and paid homage to Haman, for so the king had commanded concerning him. But Mordecai would not bow or pay homage. ³ Then the king's servants who were within the king's gate said to Mordecai, "Why do you transgress the king's command?" ⁴ Now it happened, when they spoke to him daily and he would not listen to them, that they told it to Haman, to see whether Mordecai's words would stand; for Mordecai had told them that he was a Jew. ⁵ When Haman saw that Mordecai did not bow or pay him homage, Haman was filled with wrath. ⁶ But he disdained to lay hands on Mordecai alone, for they had told him of the people of Mordecai. Instead, Haman sought to destroy all the Jews who were throughout the whole kingdom of Ahasuerus—the people of Mordecai" (Esther 3:1-6).

As an added benefit to his new position, the king also commanded all his servants and officials who were within his gate to bow down and pay homage to Haman. Everyone bowed to Haman except Mordecai, even after being urged by the other king's officials, who reminded him daily that he was transgressing the king's command. See, Mordecai was a Jew who would only bow to God in obedience to His commandments. Haman was obviously offended when he learned of Mordecai's stance. As a result, he plotted to kill not only Mordecai, but all the Jews in the kingdom.

Herod and Herodias

It was unforgiveness that motivated the murder of John the Baptist. We read in Mark 6 that John had rebuked King Herod for taking his brother Philip's wife for himself. John the Baptist, as a prophet and man of God, stood up to the king and told him outright, "It is not lawful for you to have your brother's wife." Herod certainly did not take it well, nor did Herodias, the wife in the story. In Mark 6:19, we read, "Therefore Herodias held it against him and wanted to kill him, but she could not." Both Herod and Herodias took offense at John the Baptist. Herodias could not kill him right away, so she nurtured her unforgiveness until the opportunity to carry out her evil desire toward John the Baptist presented itself. This is classic behavior for offended people. John the Baptist's offense was telling the truth that neither Herod nor Herodias wanted to hear. We see this quite often in our own lives, when we are offended by someone who tells us the truth we don't want to hear.

I remember several years ago, when I was a leader in a campus ministry, I sensed the Holy Spirit asking me to go visit a young sister who was also a member of our campus ministry. It was during my morning prayer time. We all lived on the university campus. I told God that I would do it at noon during the lunch break from the morning classes. When I came to my dorm for lunch, I had almost forgotten about the assignment, except that the Holy Spirit reminded me at the moment I was giving thanks for the food. I then told God that I would go visit her after the afternoon classes. As I dropped my backpack in my room and set out to visit my sister, I suddenly realized that the Holy Spirit had not told me the purpose of my visit. So, I quickly prayed in my heart, "Lord, you are sending me, but you have not told me the purpose of my visit. What am I supposed to say?" I was eagerly listening to the voice of God in my heart as I walked toward her dorm room. All I could hear was the word encouragement. I knew that God wanted me to encourage her. I knocked on her door, and she opened. We greeted each other and talked for a while about life and school.

At some point, I told her that I believed the Lord had sent me to come encourage her. Her immediate reaction was, "And why do you think the Lord sent you to come see me?" It came with anger. I was actually shocked by her reaction. To calm the stormy atmosphere in the room, I told her, "I did not come to offend or upset you; I thought I heard from the Lord. If that is not the case, please forgive my mistake." I left her room very disappointed and confused. I turned to the Lord and said, "Lord, I believed it was You speaking to me; now look at the mess I have caused!" For a few weeks, I was doubting the voice of God in my heart, until one day, this same sister came to me and apologized. She told me, "I know that God had sent you to speak to me that day." This young believer was slipping into sin and rebellion and did not want to hear from God at that time. She got offended the moment I mentioned that God had sent me to her. I am so grateful that, although it took some time, she got convicted, even to the point of apologizing.

Unfortunately, that was not the outcome in the case of John the Baptist. Pride and the abuse of power and authority took hold of Herod and Herodias, and they decided to kill John the Baptist.

8 THE CASE OF ESAU AND JACOB

Esau got offended by his brother, Jacob, stealing his blessing. His reaction was that he would kill his brother immediately following their father's death. He actually kept this intention and desire for a long time. The Bible does not tell us how long Jacob stayed in Padan Aram where he had fled, but it was most definitely more than the 14 years he served for his two wives, Leah and Rachel, and we need to add the fact that when he returned to Canaan, some of his children were old enough to be shepherds on their own. We are told that right after Jacob finished his farewell with Laban, who had come to harm him nonetheless, Jacob was told that his brother Esau was coming to meet him. We can surmise that Esau was not coming for a peaceful reunion with Jacob because he had 400 men with him. Why would he need 400 men? That was an army by those time's standards. Remember that Abraham had 318 men to go to war and deliver Lot (Genesis 14:14). We are also told that Jacob was afraid when he heard that his brother was coming to meet him with 400 men, because he understood his brother's intentions. Esau could have sent a messenger of peace to Jacob before meeting him, but he did not. We should understand why Jacob was afraid, to the point of confessing his fear to God. The point I am trying to get across is that Esau kept his rancor, bitterness, and desire to murder his own brother for decades (30 years would be on the lower end of this guess). Some of you reading this book can relate to this assessment.

I believe that the only thing that prevented Esau from actually killing Jacob was an encounter with God, much in the same way God encountered Laban, who was also pursuing Jacob to harm him. Of course, the Bible does not tell of God meeting Esau and telling him not to harm Jacob, but such a drastic overnight change from desiring to kill Jacob to embracing him, crying on his shoulder, and offering protection is beyond the human ability, especially for a person who has harbored unforgiveness for so long.

We would be wrong to assume or conclude that Esau's unforgiveness ended with his reunion with his brother Jacob. It did not! We read of the hatred of the descendants of Esau towards the descendants of Jacob when the latter were traveling out of the Egyptian bondage to the land God had promised them. This is more than 400, or possibly 500, years after the reunion. I see only one possibility for that to happen: Esau's unforgiveness turned to anger and hatred as usual, and then Esau transmitted the anger and hatred to his children. Let's explore some mentions and manifestations of this in the Bible.

First, we are told that the descendants of Esau would not allow the descendants of Jacob to go through their territory on their way to the promised land (Numbers 20:14–21). Second, it is not only that the descendants of Esau refused passage to the descendants of Jacob, but some of them, namely the Amalekites, actually attacked the Israelites as they were on their journey to the promised land. This must have grieved God enough to vow the complete destruction of the Amalekites (Exodus 17:14). Third, we are told that the descendants of Esau would sometimes attack the land of Israel when the latter were in calamity, in hopes of conquering their land (Obadiah 1:1–16). God actually qualifies their behavior as coming from perpetual anger and wrath kept forever (Amos 1:11–12). In Ezekiel 35:5, God tells us that this behavior of Esau's descendants stems from an ancient hatred. Pay close attention to the words that God is using: anger, wrath, and hatred. Do you wonder when, where, and how all that started? Think of the offense of the stolen blessing!

If we don't deal with unforgiveness, it will pervade our existence and consume us with the same anger, wrath, and hatred. We need to be careful not to fall into the trap of Esau, whose descendants were eventually vowed to complete destruction by God Himself through several prophets. The danger is that once unforgiveness has spread around, eventually reaching the next generation, it becomes impossible to stop or reverse.

Unfortunately, this level of unforgiveness that evolves into generational hatred is not isolated to the case of Esau and Jacob. When we look at the world today, we see hatred towards innocent people who have nothing to do with the causes for which they're being hated. Families and nations have been torn apart, with the people on one side of the conflict not talking to the people on the other side and their descendants for the longest time. Wars have been and are still being fought today, and genocides have happened, all because of generational unforgiveness. Think about the descendants of a certain tribe or race being hated because of the offenses of their forefathers.

The point is clear: we quite often spread our unforgiveness to others around us and recruit them to join us in our offended atmosphere and hatred of the offenders. However close a relationship you may have with an offended person, don't take their offense against an offender that did not offend you directly. You will fall into the trap and sin of hating someone without a cause (Matthew 5:22).

9 GOD'S PERSPECTIVE

It is important for us to realize how God views and weighs offenses. Our sins against God are the 10,000 talents and more that we cannot and could never repay, and the offenses we suffer from people are the 100 denarii or less. I am not trying to lessen the severity or the amount of pain people incur through offenses. What I am trying to say is that a single sin against God cannot be repaid, and there is nothing you can do to earn forgiveness from God. Remember what the expert at the law of God came to ask Jesus, testing Him in Luke 10:25, "What shall I do to inherit eternal life?" The answer is not in the things or the amount of things you can do (actions, works).

The Bible teaches us that the salvation of our souls is costly (Psalm 49:8) and that there is no amount of wealth that is worth the value of the soul (Matt 16:26). We could never repay God the debt we owe Him. Salvation is a free gift from God through our Lord and Savior, Jesus Christ. The price that we could not pay, Jesus paid by offering His own life as a ransom. In other words, the amount of debt you and I owe God because of our sins has the value of Jesus's life in God's value system. Maybe you don't value your life or anyone else's as much, but remember that Jesus is the only begotten Son of God. How much do you think God values the life of His only begotten Son? If there is no price on earth to value your soul, how about Jesus's? God is a rich God. He lacks no resources. He owns all the riches and wealth—all the diamonds, all the gold, all the precious metals—not only on earth, not only on all the planets and moons of our solar system, not only in our Milky Way galaxy, but in all the universe. God could have paid the ransom for your soul and mine in silver, gold, diamonds, or any other precious stones or metals, in quantities that only He could determine, because He owns an endless supply of these. Instead, God determined that the only price for our redemption or ransom was the value of the life of Jesus Christ, His only begotten Son, His most precious and valuable possession. We must realize how great a debt we owed God, and thus, how much He has forgiven us, and that He did and still does it out of love. God paid this debt regardless of the severity of our sin. However small or great our sin or sins may be in our own valuation, God still paid the same price.

Also, He paid it in advance. The Bible teaches us in Revelation 13:8 that the Lamb of God was slain (sacrificed) before the foundation of the world. Also, in Romans 5:8, the apostle Paul tells us that Christ died for us (for our salvation) while we were still sinners. We understand that Christ died for us, i.e., God paid the price for our salvation, redemption, ransom, and forgiveness, even before all of us since the second century were born, with the exception of the few people who outlived Him in the first century and made it into the second century. We must also realize that the debt people owe us through the offenses they have caused us does not amount, not even close, to what we owe God.

10 WOUNDS OF THE HEART

The next question I usually ask when teaching on this subject is if anyone has a scar on their body. Everyone usually says yes. I then ask everyone to touch the scar, press on it, and tell us if there is any pain. This may sound silly, but the reality is that although the scars still carry all the memory of the physical wound and even its pain, the wound itself has been healed a long time ago, and its memory does not hurt. We must understand that offenses are what I call "wounds of the heart." And the same process of healing that is applied to physical wounds can also be applied to these wounds of the heart, except with different ingredients or by a different physician.

We get physical wounds under different circumstances, some of which are completely outside of our control, and some from our own mistakes. But regardless of how we get wounded, we have all come to know the process of treating the wound. First, we must apply pressure to the wound to stop the bleeding. Even though the pressure itself increases the pain, failure to stop the bleeding has more dire consequences. So, we absorb the extra pain from the pressure because it is part of the healing process. Second, the wound has to be cleaned. Third, some medication may be needed. Fourth, wrapping or bandaging (protection from foreign agents, potential infectors) may be necessary, and finally, time. This is when the immune system and your own body work to heal the wound. This last part is internal, designed by God Himself. In other words, God Himself is at work in the healing process.

If not treated properly and promptly, the wound will get infected, the problem will become worse and even more painful, and it will take even longer to heal, if it even heals at all. There are stories of infected wounds that could have been treated and healed, but the lack of adequate treatment eventually led to amputations.

11 YOU CANNOT FORGIVE FROM A WOUNDED HEART

I still remember a good friend's reaction just a few years ago when I was teaching a small group Bible study on this subject of forgiveness. He flatly said, "I will never forgive them for what they have done to me." Most of you have probably heard such statements, and some of you have probably uttered such statements. To be honest, I was a little surprised, and kind of disappointed to hear my friend say that. After all, he was a mature believer, loved Jesus, and was actively involved in the church, serving in various capacities along with his wife and children. The first question that went through my mind was, "Are you not aware of what Jesus told the disciples about the lack or failure to forgive?" Yet I could not deny his genuine faith and love for the Lord. That is when I understood the real problem, which affects most believers struggling with forgiveness. It is not that they are not aware of Jesus's or the apostles' teachings on forgiveness. It is rather the lack of understanding of the process of forgiveness and where it proceeds from.

The first thing you and we must realize is that we cannot forgive from a hurt and wounded heart. This is very important, because we tend to turn forgiveness into an emotional issue. It is true that Jesus taught that forgiveness must proceed from the heart (Matthew 18:35). But when you have been offended, especially deeply so, even your feelings toward the offender are hurt. So, the same feelings cannot turn around from the hurting state. When we are hurting from an offense, every feeling towards and thought about the offender is negative. Let's be honest, we just feel like the offender should pay for their offense. We are fully aware that we should forgive, but every thought of the offense and the offender is just too painful to even think about forgiving. So, we fall into the second pain of guilt, knowing that we should forgive, but finding ourselves neither able nor willing to forgive.

The basic principle I am trying to establish here is that forgiveness does not proceed from a wounded heart. The reason you find it hard or impossible to forgive is because you are hurt, and a wounded and hurt heart cannot forgive. Actually, a wounded and hurt heart is a dangerous heart, because it tends to spread the hurt and the offense. As I wrote earlier, it drags other people into the hurt and the offense who would otherwise have no connection with the offense. A wounded and hurting heart tends to hurt other people. That's why a wounded and hurting heart must be healed.

12 LACK OF UNDERSTANDING

There is a second reason why it is difficult to forgive as a believer that stems from a lack of understanding of God's forgiveness. Jesus and the apostles taught us to forgive as God forgives. Yes, Jesus taught and expects us, the professing believers in Jesus Christ, the saved and redeemed by the blood of the Lamb of God, to forgive as God forgives. The apostle Paul wrote, " ... forgiving one another, even as God in Christ forgave you" (Ephesians 4:32). Since we must forgive as God forgives, we must understand how God forgives. There is a lot to be said about God's forgiveness. But besides the trivial task of defining the nature and essence of forgiveness, I have come to the understanding that there are three words that characterize God's forgiveness: love, immediate, and permanent.

We all know the verse that says "God is love," so it is easy to understand that God forgives out of love. But most believers struggle with God's forgiveness being immediate and permanent. How many believers continue to confess the same sin to God over and over again, after they have genuinely repented, just because they don't believe that God has already forgiven them? I want to illustrate these two characteristics of God's forgiveness through the familiar story of David and Bathsheba, as recounted in 2 Samuel, chapters 11 and 12. Please read those two chapters before continuing to read what follows. Doing so will not only refresh your memory of the story, but it will also give you a better understanding of what I am about to explain.

In this story, we see the horrible sins that David committed. He covets someone else's wife, commits adultery with her, abuses his power and position as king, conceals his adultery, basically executes Uri the husband of Bathsheba, and conceals the murder. The Bible clearly says that all that David did "displeased the Lord" (2 Samuel 11:27). Think of all the commandments that David broke in the process! You would think that someone who loves the Lord and serves the Lord with all his heart would not fall so low, but David did, and all of us are capable of the worst sins if we are not careful to watch and pray, as Jesus reminded Peter in Matthew 26:41 when he said, "...the spirit is willing, but the flesh is weak."

God sent the prophet Nathan to confront David. Eventually, David was convicted of sin and repented. Psalm 51 tells us about not only the repentance, but the agony and misery of David's soul while he hid his sins. In Psalm 32, David describes the joy of forgiveness from these very sins. Yes, after David was confronted by Nathan, convicted of his sins, and repented, God did forgive David.

Immediate

I want to draw your attention to a couple of lines in Psalm 32 and 2 Samuel 12. In Psalm 32, David writes, "I acknowledged my sin to You, And my iniquity I have not hidden. I said, "I will confess my transgressions to the LORD," And You forgave the iniquity of my sin. Selah" (Psalm 32:5). We do lose something in the translation of this verse from the original Hebrew language. Not that the translation is wrong, but the original reading would read, "… the very moment that I acknowledged my sin to You, … You forgave the iniquity of my sin." Did you hear that? David is basically saying that God forgave him immediately, the very minute he acknowledged and confessed his sin. The first time I heard a preacher mention this, I almost did not believe it, so I did what the Berean Christians did: I went to the scriptures to reread the story and find out for myself.

Let me take you back to the story in 2 Samuel 12. In verse 13, David acknowledges to Nathan, "I have sinned against the Lord." Interestingly enough, in the very next verse, Nathan, who in this case is the mouthpiece of God, says to David, "The Lord also has put away your sin." In other words, within the same verse, David confesses his sin, and God forgives him. No wonder David ends the verse in Psalm 32:5 with the word Selah, which invites the reader to pause and think (in meditation or contemplation) about what they have just read. Here we see the forgiveness of God in action, immediately.

Actually, we find this immediate forgiveness from God very early in the Bible, in Numbers 14. The story in this chapter is very well known. It tells of the time when the children of Israel failed to trust God for being able to take them to the promised land after they had spied the land and found it flowing with milk and honey as God had said, yet having giants they thought they would never be able to overcome. The people then complained to their leaders, Moses and Aaron, and decided to elect other leaders that would take them back to Egypt, despite having witnessed all the miracles God performed, not only in Egypt, but also through their journey in the wilderness up to this point in time. The people even tried to stone Caleb and Joshua, the only two spies who believed and tried to reassure the congregation that God could help them conquer the land. This once-more episode and level of unbelief angered God to the point that He was willing to destroy the entire congregation and start afresh with Moses (verses 11–12). But Moses reasoned and pleaded with God, and he concluded his plea by asking God to pardon the people (verse 19). God responded to Moses's plea right away by saying in verse 20, "I have pardoned." In other words, God did not wait or waste time. His forgiveness was granted within seconds of Moses asking, during the same conversation.

Permanent

We must also understand that God's forgiveness is permanent, meaning that when God forgives an offense, sin, or transgression, He will never take that forgiveness back. A better way to say this is that when God forgives, He also forgets—not out of forgetfulness, but because He chooses not to remember the transgression or sin. This is found in Jeremiah 31:31–34 and repeated in Hebrews 8:12, 10:17. Of course, we are familiar with the verses in Psalm 103 where God removes our transgressions from us as far as the east is from the west. I am no rocket scientist, but I know that the East and the West are so far apart from each other that they will never meet; one will never catch the other. When God forgives, He makes it impossible for your forgiven sins to catch up with you. In Jeremiah 50:20, the Lord says, "In those days and in that time," says the LORD, "the iniquity of Israel shall be sought, but there shall be none; And the sins of Judah, but they shall not be found; For I will pardon those whom I preserve."

You can walk tall and rejoice as David did in Psalm 32, because there is no more shame, guilt, or condemnation. Praise God for His grace and mercy.

Love

Now, we can all confess that we are not capable of this type of forgiveness, because this forgiveness flows from love. After all, it is love that forgives (1 Corinthians 13), and God forgives out of love, because God is love (1 John 4:8). That brings us to the next reason why we struggle with unforgiveness: we struggle to forgive because we don't love, and we don't love because love is not in us in the first place. Since we are to forgive as God forgives, the obvious conclusion when we struggle to forgive is that we do not have love–at least not God's type of love. I will spend some time elaborating on this aspect, because love is the key. Think, for example, of what Jesus commanded: to love your enemies, which includes your offenders.

Remember, the Bible teaches us that, as believers, we were once God's enemies, and He forgave us. Why? Because He loves us. And God never asks us to do what He does not, cannot, or is not willing to do Himself. Whatever God asks us to do, we can be sure that He will show us how He Himself does it. In the case at hand, God has shown us numerous times in the Scriptures how He loves and how He forgives. The problem is our unwillingness to follow God's examples and teachings.

The realization that we don't have God's love is actually a good thing. It draws us closer to God when we ask Him to fill us with His love. At this point, forgiveness is no longer about the offender.

13 FORGIVENESS AND LOVE

Forgiveness is connected to love in two ways in the Bible. I will call these the forward and the backward connections. The forward connection is established in 1 Corinthians 13: "love forgives all things." This is a blank statement that is not open for debate. It is also unconditional, as there are no dependence clauses attached to it. Most of us would love to add an "it depends" clause to this statement, but the Bible does not. We have already established that God forgives out of love. When a sinner turns to God in repentance, God does not analyze the person's life to pick and choose what sin to forgive or not. He forgives all sins. In fact, Psalm 103:3 tells us that God forgives all of our iniquities. So, the forward connection between love and forgiveness is unquestionable: love forgives, God is love, and we know God forgives.

In Luke 7:41–44, Jesus tells the story of a master who forgave the debts of two debtors: to one he forgave 500 denarii, and to the other, he forgave 50. He then asked which of the two debtors would love the master more. The obvious answer was the one to whom the master forgave the most. Here we see Jesus establishing the backward connection: love as a response to forgiveness. I mentioned earlier that we must realize how much God has forgiven and still forgives us. This is important because it establishes, or rather determines, how much we love God in return, and thus how much we love ourselves and others. Remember the great commandment?

Jesus told this story in the context of two different attitudes towards sin. One attitude was that of a Pharisee who did not think much of his sins. In fact, the Pharisee thought he was following God's law so closely that he was not much of a sinner and thus needed no forgiveness or savior. The second attitude was that of a woman who was known to the entire city to be a sinner. This woman was fully aware of her sins. She was probably just waiting for an opportunity to meet Jesus in person. She was an outcast who was not invited to the Pharisee's dinner, but nothing could stop her from getting to meet Jesus. When she got into His presence, she began weeping at His feet, washing His feet with her tears and wiping them with her own hair, and finally kissing His feet and anointing them with a very costly perfume. Jesus said that all the love she was showing was in response to forgiveness. Do not be mistaken: her weeping, wiping, kissing, and anointing did not earn her the forgiveness of her sins, because God's forgiveness cannot be earned. It is the other way around. She understood how much she had been forgiven. She knew her own sin had made her an outcast in the city, yet here was a man who, though righteous, did not reject her and even allowed her to touch Him. The self-righteous Pharisees would not allow her to touch them because of her known sins. The weight of her guilt and condemnation of her sin was lifted the moment she realized that Jesus did not reject her but actually welcomed her. She understood she was loved. Again, it is love that forgives. So, all that she did was only a response to the love and forgiveness she received in the first place, and that love and its forgiveness birthed love in her soul, for Jesus said that all that she did was showing love. I call her love a response love, which is a love that is in response to being loved and forgiven.

We see here that love forgives. So, when we don't forgive, or if we struggle to, it means we don't love, or at least we don't have that type of love in us. This means we don't realize or know how much God loves us and has forgiven us in the first place, if indeed we have come to Him with a humble and repenting heart, asking for our own forgiveness. In short, we struggle to forgive because we don't know or have God's love.

14 GOD'S LOVE

Where do we even start to write about or describe God's love? I am reminded of the hymn, "The Love of God," by Frederick M. Lehman (1917):

The love of God is greater far
Than tongue or pen can ever tell;
It goes beyond the highest star,
And reaches to the lowest hell;
The guilty pair, bowed down with care,
God gave His Son to win;
His erring child He reconciled,
And pardoned from his sin.

Refrain:
Oh, love of God, how rich and pure!
How measureless and strong!
It shall forevermore endure—
The saints' and angels' song.

When hoary time shall pass away,
And earthly thrones and kingdoms fall,
When men who here refuse to pray,
On rocks and hills and mountains call,
God's love so sure, shall still endure,
All measureless and strong;

Redeeming grace to Adam's race—
The saints' and angels' song.

Could we with ink the ocean fill,
And were the skies of parchment made,
Were every stalk on earth a quill,
And every man a scribe by trade;
To write the love of God above
Would drain the ocean dry;
Nor could the scroll contain the whole,
Though stretched from sky to sky.

There is no one word that is adequate enough to describe God's love. It is the purest thing one can ever find, the most precious and most awesome. The love of God is not only wonderful, it is also generous, abundant, captivating, and powerful yet gentle enough to move the hardest heart. It is comforting, reassuring, and encouraging. It is available to all, and it will never run out. If I apply the lines of 1 Corinthians 13:4–8 to the love of God, they would read like this: (The) love (of God) suffers long and is kind; (the) love (of God) does not envy; (the) love (of God) does not parade itself, is not puffed up; does not behave rudely, does not seek its own, is not provoked, thinks no evil; does not rejoice in iniquity, but rejoices in the truth; bears all things, believes all things, hopes all things, endures all things. (The) love (of God) never fails...

We are all familiar with the most known verse of the Bible, John 3:16, "For God so loved the world that He gave His only begotten Son, that whoever believes in Him should not perish but have everlasting life." The construction of this verse implies that the amount of love God has for the world in general, and every single human being in particular, could only be valued by the life of Jesus, His only begotten Son. Jesus told us in Matthew 6:31, "Wherever your treasure is, your heart will be also." We set our hearts or love on the things and people we value. How many spouses have felt unloved and abandoned because the other spouse spent so much time on their hobby?

I mentioned this earlier when discussing the ratio of debts, and it is worth repeating here: God values every single human being exactly as He values Jesus Christ, His only begotten Son. This is mind-blowing, that a perfectly pure, holy, and righteous God would value flawed, sinful, ignorant, rebellious, depraved, and immoral human beings as much as He values His perfectly pure, holy, and righteous only Son, His most precious possession. And because God values us that much, He also loves us that much. Jesus made this connection in his sacerdotal prayer in John 17:26. In the entire chapter of John 17, Jesus is praying for His disciples. In verse 26, He adds the concept that underscores our discussion. This is what He said at the end of the prayer, meaning the closing line of the prayer: "And I have declared to them Your name, and will declare it, that the love with which You loved Me may be in them, and I in them." In other words, Jesus prayed that the same love that God the Father had for Him, the only begotten Son, would also be in the disciples. Now we also know that God always hears and answers Jesus. Therefore, we can be sure that God answered this prayer, even though we don't seem to experience it, much like many other promises of God. But I want every disciple of Jesus to know, whether you feel it or not, experience it or not, understand it or not, that God loves you just as much as He loves Jesus. By the way, this is not the only time Jesus introduces this concept. He also said to the disciples in John 15:9, "As the Father loved me, I also have loved you." So not only did Jesus pray that God the Father would love us with the same love the Father has for God the Son, Jesus himself loves us with the same love the Father has for Him.

I know I said earlier that God values every human being as He values Jesus, and He also loves every human being, disciple or not, just as He loves Christ. We read in Romans 5:8, "God demonstrates His own love towards us, in that while we were still sinners, Christ died for us." In other words, God's love for the believer does not begin at conversion; it does not begin at the moment a sinner repents and turns to God. That love is only discovered and fully experienced in the confined context of a relationship with Jesus Christ as His fully surrendered disciple. See, outside of the disciple-and-savior relationship, a person cannot fully experience God's forgiveness, because it requires repentance toward God and faith in Christ as their personal Lord and Savior.

When a person is touched by this overwhelming, unconditional, unending, all-consuming, and all-sufficient love, a reaction like that of the sinful woman we just talked about is no longer strange; it becomes normal and insufficient at the same time. We wish we could do more to show our love and gratitude, but we are faced with the limitations of human nature and the immensity of God's love. No praise, worship, or adoration is enough, and words fail us as we try to ascribe worth and glory to God.

15 DO I HAVE THIS LOVE

You may ask, I am a disciple of Jesus Christ; why am I not experiencing this love?" This is a fair and important question, because the answer to the question may unlock your ability to forgive. First of all, you need to examine your heart, especially the extent of your surrender and submission to God and His word, and how you live it out. Second, you need to examine the extent to which you believe what the word of God says He has already done for you. You will need the Spirit of God to open your understanding of your identity in Christ, your blessings from God through Jesus Christ, your value and worth in God's eyes, and just how much He loves you, as Jesus prayed. Last but not least, you need to appropriate this piece of Scripture in Romans 5:5, "... the love of God has been poured out in our hearts by the Holy Spirit who was given to us." Here, the apostle Paul is teaching the disciples in Rome that this incredible and indescribable love of God has been poured out in our hearts, apparently without conditions, so it is already in the heart of the believer in Christ. Do you believe it?

One thing I understand about the verb "to pour" is that it implies the emptying of the content of one vessel into another, either completely or partially, and the quantity that was poured into the receiving vessel does not remain in the pouring vessel. To me, this verse means that God took the container of His love, which is His heart, and emptied it partially into my heart. He did not empty it completely into my heart, because His love cannot run dry, and besides, there has to be some for you, too. Whether you believe that as a disciple of Christ this love of God has been poured out in your heart is up to you. However, failing to believe this, which results in failing to live in this love, is a significant hindrance to your relationship with God. Just like the sinful woman in Luke 7 did, you can choose to pour this love back on God, or you can choose to hold it back. Personally, I have come to realize that the more I pour back on God through worship and service, the more I feel refilled with the same love, and the cycle does not stop. Likewise, when I spend days without communing with God in His presence, my heart and my soul begin to feel empty and dry, and I need to run back into God's presence.

Look carefully at the sentence construction: ... the love of God has been poured out into our hearts by the Holy Spirit. It has been, meaning it is already done from God's perspective. So, when the believer in Christ does not feel this love, or feels like they do not have this love of God in their heart, the first thing to question is the openness of their heart to God's love. This is because the pouring out is one thing, but the receiving into our hearts is another thing. The vessel that the love is being poured into must be open to receiving what is being poured. Otherwise, the content being poured is wasted and lost. God does not want to waste His love.

There is a second requirement for receiving God's love. Besides your heart being open, you must also be in the position of receiving. See, when you pour anything from one vessel into another, position matters, and that is for both vessels. I believe God is already positioned to pour His love, but I doubt that we are always positioned to receive it. This makes me think of the story in the Old Testament (2 Kings 4), where a prophet died and left a widow and orphans with debt. The widow went to explain her plight to Elisha the prophet, who told her to go and gather empty bottles and vessels from neighbors, shut the door behind her, and pour the little oil that she had left into the borrowed bottles and vessels. Anytime this poor widow grabbed an empty vessel, positioned it properly, and took the action to pour oil into the empty vessel from her only jar, a miracle happened: she filled the receiving vessel, but her jar was not emptied, so she picked another vessel to pour oil into until all the vessels were filled. She was able to sell the "miracle oil," pay all the debts the late husband had, and live on the leftover money. We have to be empty of ourselves, open, and positioned to receive the love of God into our hearts.

The openness and position of the hearts are why many believers do not feel the love of God to the fullest. They feel God loves some believers more than themselves and others, as if God has favorites. I usually tease some friends at my local church that I am God's favorite, and the onus is on them to prove me wrong. Seriously, though, we have to be honest with ourselves. Do you feel like God loves others more than you, or do you feel like only trickles of God's love reach your heart and not its streams or waves? Allow me to say that you may have a connection or capacity problem, the solution to which can be very simple depending on your attitude.

This is how I usually illustrate the problem when I teach about this aspect of the love of God. Imagine that you have in your house an electrical outlet into which you plug a microwave oven and a cell phone. Due to their own capacities, these two devices will draw different amounts of electric power from the same outlet. Mind you, the outlet has the same voltage and amperage potential available to any device that it can feed. The microwave will draw a lot more power from the outlet than the cellphone. The problem is not in the outlet; it does not discriminate. Likewise, many believers are plugged into the outlet of God's love at the cellphone level, drawing only a little bit of God's love, while other believers have learned to plug into the outlet of God's love as a microwave oven. I mentioned that this is due to their capacities. What is your capacity to consume God's love? This question is answered by the degree of hunger and thirst for God you nurture and also by how much of God's love you consume by extending it to the people around you. Does this love flow from you? If yes, then God does not mind refilling your heart. Are you plugged in, i.e., connected to this outlet?

There is a story of an elderly couple who had always wanted to travel on a cruise but did not have the money to pay for the tickets. They managed to save money over the years to finally afford the tickets. When trip time came, they packed their suitcases with clothes and essentials, which included a load of peanut butter crackers. At meal time during the cruise, while every passenger went to eat in one of the dinner halls, the old couple went into their cabin and sat down to eat peanut butter crackers, with the smell of the delicious foods that the other passengers were enjoying wafting through their room. They dreamed they could also enjoy those meals. Towards the end of the trip, a fellow church member who was also traveling on the cruise noticed that she had not seen the old couple in the dinner halls at any meal time. She went to chat with them and could not help but ask why she had not seen them at meal time. The answer from the couple was that they only paid for the ticket and had no money left to pay for the meals, so they packed crackers, and that is what they had been secretly eating in their cabin. The fellow church member went on to explain to this old couple that their ticket price included all their meals during the trip, and they could enjoy the meals in the dinner halls like everyone else. I am glad that they got to eat some of those delicious cruise meals before the trip was over. Yet, I can't help but wonder how many believers in Christ live this Christian life like that old couple. The most abundant, lavish, and delicious buffet of God's love has been paid for and is available, yet, the Christian is surviving on crackers, watching others eat their fill.

16 IN HIS PRESENCE

The openness and emptiness refer to the condition of your heart, while the positioning refers to getting into the presence of God. Have you ever been in the presence of God? Do you know how to get into His presence? When was the last time you felt like you were in the presence of God? Those who have ever been in the presence of God know that it is an experience that is very hard to describe in words, yet it leaves one with a feeling of awe, wonder, and security all at once, like a little child wrapped in the arms of a loving and caring parent. All the worries vanish—the fears, stress, anxiety, problems, and troubles of life. You forget about yourself, and you even forget about having enemies and offenders; you just soak in this wonderful moment, and, like Peter on the mount of transfiguration (Matthew 12, Mark 9), your only desire is to dwell there. This is also what Mary did while Martha, her sister, was busy with all the logistics of receiving Jesus as a guest. We are all too busy to take the time that is necessary to enter God's presence. We are distracted by a million things in this life. Yet, we must cultivate what Brother Lawrence termed "the practice of the presence of God."

The Bible says, "In His presence there is fullness of joy" (Psalm 16:11). Jesus himself said that He wants His disciples to have joy and that their joy may be full (John 15:1, 16:24). The fullness of that joy is found in the presence of God.

We need to understand that the most holy place, also called the holy of holies, was that place in the tabernacle where the ark of the covenant was located. It was overshadowed with two cherubim and separated from the holy place by a thick veil. That way, no person ministering in the holy place could see anything in the most holy place except the ends of the poles that were used to carry the arc of the covenant whenever the children of Israel moved from one place to another and had to re-erect the tabernacle. It is in this holy place that God's presence was found, for God Himself had told Moses in Exodus 25:22 that that is where He would meet with him. Anytime God wanted to meet with Moses or Moses wanted to meet with God, it was at the tabernacle of meeting, and God would speak from the most holy place. No one had access to the most holy place except the high priest, and even he could only go there once a year. Any person who randomly ventured in there outside of the appointed time would fall dead on the spot, even if it were the high priest himself, not to mention the other priests, the Levites, or the common people. Even the priest did not haphazardly walk into the most holy place at the appointed time. He was supposed to be dressed in his anointed ministry garments. He would also have offered the sacrifices for sins—one for himself and one for the people. He would then enter the holy place; walk past the lampstand, the table of showbread, and the incense altar; then walk past the veil into the most holy place to present the blood of the sacrifice.

We are told in the Bible that when Jesus died on the cross, the veil that separated the holy place from the most holy place, i.e., the very presence of God, was torn from top to bottom (Matthew 27:21, Mark 15:38, Luke 23:45). Now, not only can anyone in the holy place see the most holy place, but the restriction that allowed only the high priest to go into the most holy place once a year has been lifted. In 1 Peter 2:9, the apostle quotes Exodus 19:6 where God speaks concerning Israel that they would be to Him "a kingdom of priests." It has always been God intention that believers should and would worship Him from the holy place where on priest could enter, and better yet, from the most holy place. It is sad to see that even in this day and age, with all the understanding of Scriptures and all the books that have been written, most Christians continue to worship God from the "temple's courtyard". We must understand and appropriate the fact that Jesus's sacrifice on the cross has made a way for every believer, not just a select few, to access the presence of God and enjoy the flowing streams of His love, mercy, grace, and compassion that He makes new every morning in His great faithfulness. It is in His presence that safety and security are found.

In Psalm 23:4, David said, "Yeah, though I walk through the valley of the shadow of death, I will fear no evil, for you are with me ..." David begins this verse with what I call a shout of confidence: Yeah. He then tells us that he is confident that he can walk through the valley of the shadow of death. Think about the valley where he confidently walked toward and eventually killed Goliath. Finally, he gives us the reason for his confidence: the presence of God. He says, "for you are with me." In Psalm 56:11, this same David, being confident of God's presence by his side, asked the rhetorical question after declaring his trust in the Lord and that he will not be afraid, "What can man do to me?"

See, living and walking, or just being in the presence of God, even for one moment, is life-changing. It is in this presence that the love of God enraptures you; it is where the whisper of His voice into your spirit becomes clear and brings healing, comfort, and understanding. It is in His presence that you truly "taste and see that the Lord is good," as none else but David tells us in Psalm 34:8. It is also there where you begin to see things from God's perspective. This presence fills your heart and soul with peace—not just any peace, but the peace of God, which surpasses all understanding, as the apostle Paul said in Philippians 4:7. This is where you find rest for your soul, as Jesus said in Matthew 11:29, and where your soul is restored, as David said in Psalm 23:3. Here, you become as confident as David, you know that with God's presence, you can face any giant, and you will come out victorious from any battle.

The good news is that we can enter His presence anytime and anywhere, regardless of our surroundings or circumstances. Jesus himself promised to be with us always (Matthew 28:20). So, we are guaranteed His presence. How come we don't feel it and even doubt it? My guess is because we don't take the time to enter into it. His presence is available, but we must enter it. Look at Jesus being in the house with Mary and Martha (Luke 10:38–42). While Mary understood the importance of being in His presence, Martha was like every one of us, busy with the cares of life. His presence is still available today. Have you ever been in the presence of God? If not, ask God to draw you into His presence. We must seek His face continually, as David exhorts us in Psalm 105:4 (see also 1 Chronicles 16:11).

17 SOME EXAMPLES IN THE BIBLE

I think of Job, a man richly blessed and protected by God, but whose riches, possessions, children, and health Satan attacked and destroyed. Pain, anguish, sorrow, and distress destroyed his appearance, so much so that his close friends could not recognize him. Job went through a series of questions, seeking to understand why these calamities befell him, because nothing made sense, not even God. See, at that time, the common understanding of God (the theology of the time) was that God blessed the righteous and punished the wicked. Yet here was a righteous man suffering calamity upon calamity. To make matters worse, all of the close friends who were supposed to bring some comfort and relief began to accuse him of having sinned and hiding it. What a betrayal! How offensive can that be?

But Job sought God's face to present and plead his case. In other words, he was seeking God's presence. When God finally shows up and Job finally gets in the presence of God, he recants his questions, forgets about himself and his pain, and is awestruck not only by the glory and majesty of God but much more by His wisdom and depth of knowledge. We usually focus on the restoration part of Job's story, which is fine. But I want to draw your attention to the fact that all of Job's questions and concerns, his depression, and his suicidal thoughts vanished in the presence of God. He was healed, not just physically but also emotionally. He forgave the friends who had betrayed and offended him, praying for their own restoration. This is exactly the opposite of what we would do to and for our offenders. But Job did it because he was healed and restored in the presence of God.

Asaph, the author of Psalm 73, gives a similar theme. He considers the prosperity and wellbeing of the wicked and the arrogance of the proud, to the point where he becomes envious of the boastful and regrets having lived a godly life. In essence, things did not make sense; it was the world upside down, and it had become too painful for Asaph to try to understand or explain. We don't know how long that lasted. The question is repeated many times in the book of Psalms, and this one seems to summarize them: LORD, how long will the wicked, How long will the wicked triumph (Psalm 94:3)? As for Asaph, the end to the questioning came, and things began to make sense when he went into the sanctuary, in the presence of God (Psalm 73:17).

We should all not only desire to be in God's presence; we should be desperate for it. How? As the dry and parched ground from a drought longs for the rain, and as the deer pants for water (Psalm 42:1-2). We have such an opportunity to enter God's presence! The invitation is freely extended, and the door is open. God is waiting for us with open arms. However, there are two obstacles we must overcome: sin and our self-confidence/self-reliance.

How do I know I am in God's presence, or how do I get into His presence? This is actually simpler than most people think. Remember that God is everywhere, always. Jesus promised to be with us always. So, the most important thing I do to get into His presence is to turn my attention to Him, and by that, I mean focusing on Him. This focus can take many forms: reading the Bible, praying, praising and worshiping, or just meditating on His word. The key point here is that my mind and my thoughts are undividedly focused on Him. At some point, my spirit begins to commune with His Spirit. The problem that most of us face is that we do all these things rather regularly, but we don't get into His presence because we are not focused on Him. We praise God while we are thinking about many other things; we read the Bible, but we are not focused on getting what God may be wanting to teach us through the lines we are reading because our hearts are not prepared for meditating on His word. Sometimes we focus on Him, but we don't linger long enough in His presence to begin to commune with His Spirit and hear Him, or the routine spiritual disciplines just become mechanical.

18 PERSONAL STORIES

I want to share two examples of how important it is for us to get into God's presence.

The first example happened during a family vacation trip not long ago. After arriving at our destination, we settled in our lodging place, which had all the amenities of modern life. One morning, I snuck out of bed to pray and meditate, and believe it or not, to continue writing this book. When my wife woke up, she also wanted to pray. She usually gets into God's presence through worship. This morning, however, the internet service was down, and she could not play her favorite worship songs that usher her into God's presence. I suggested she just sing the songs. That suggestion almost devolved into an argument between her and me, something that would not have happened had she already been in God's presence.

The second example happened many years ago when I was in graduate school in Grenoble, France. Lucien, a good friend of mine and fellow native of Cameroon, was also studying at the same university. We lived in the same dorm, on the same second floor of a 5-story dorm building, and attended the same campus ministry. He was traveling back to Cameroon and had to catch a flight in Paris. It was at the Paris airport where he realized he had forgotten his passport in his dorm room in Grenoble, with the flight to Cameroon scheduled to leave in 6 hours. Fortunately, he had left the key to his dorm room with me. I remember receiving a call from

Lucien that morning around 7 a.m., telling me he forgot his passport in his room and giving instructions on how to retrieve it. He had also called another friend named Lucas, who had a car, and gave him instructions on how to ship the passport to him at the Paris airport from the regional airport in Grenoble. I thought to myself, this is easy, since all I have to do is open his room, get the passport, and hand it to Lucas when he shows up, then go to class.

The problem was that by 8 a.m., Lucas had not shown up, and I had not heard back from Lucien either. A few minutes later, the phone rang, and it was Lucien calling to tell me that Lucas was not going to do it, so he was asking me to take his passport to the Grenoble regional airport and ship it to him. As a broke student on a Cameroon government scholarship that was not disbursed regularly, I grabbed my wallet and checkbook, in which there was only one check left, and in my wallet was 100 French francs, the equivalent of $20 at the time. I made a quick calculation in my mind that the 100 French francs was enough to pay for my ride to the regional airport and back, and I would pay the fees for shipping the passport with the only check left in my checkbook.

I arrived at the bus station to find out the one-way fare to the airport was 60 French francs. I paid it anyway, because I had to ship this passport to my desperate friend in Paris. As I sat in that bus on the way to the airport, suddenly a series of questions popped into my mind: will this operation succeed? Will you be able to ship this passport? Will it get to Lucien? Doubts and fear began to flood my soul. I remember saying to myself within my heart, "Let me turn to the Holy Spirit to see what He would say." So, I engaged in this conversation with the Holy Spirit, and I asked Him flatly, "Holy Spirit, will this work? Will I succeed in shipping this passport to Lucien?" The answer that I heard in my heart was a resounding and emphatic "Yes, it will work." How I know that this response was from the Holy Spirit is the subject of another book, but I want to say here that the passport was shipped to Lucien, which was nothing short of a miracle, given all the difficulties I faced at the airport.

The message I am conveying through this story is that stepping into God's presence in the midst of chaos, doubts, and fears allows you to hear from God, and once you have heard from Him, you can latch your faith on His word. Oh, I forgot one important detail: that very morning, before the first call from Lucien came in, I had asked God in my devotion and prayer time to increase my faith. Little did I know the adventure that He had prepared. I could have succumbed to my fears and doubts and given up, and that would have canceled my friend's trip. But turning to the Holy Spirit, stepping into God's presence, allowed me to hear from Him and believe Him, which resulted in me (and Lucien) witnessing a miracle. Some crises are awaiting a person who can spend time in the presence of God and be used as His instrument for the solution.

19 BACK TO LOVE

Why does God make His presence available to us? The answer is simple: because He loves us. How great a love (Ephesians 3:19)!

The apostle Paul is well qualified to tell and teach us about the greatness of God's love. He was a bright and learned man, and he was a perfect disciple of Judaism. When Jesus meets him on his way to Damascus with further plans to persecute the church, He asks him bluntly, "Saul, Saul, why are you persecuting Me?" Notice that by persecuting the church, Saul of Tarsus, who later becomes the apostle Paul, is persecuting Jesus Himself, and this is according to Jesus. By his actions, Saul had positioned himself as an enemy of Jesus. Yet, he saw this love transform the former church persecutor and chief sinner (by his own words, 1 Timothy 1:15) that he was. It is this man who tells us that the love of God cannot be measured and is beyond knowledge (Ephesians 3:19). How did he come to such a conclusion? He experienced the love of God, and as a learned and intelligent man, he found that it surpasses whatever knowledge we may have or have experienced of the love of God, and there is still more to discover about it. Maybe you have stalled in your knowledge of the love of God. I pray God will reveal more of His love to you and for you.

Why did I spend time talking about God's love in our hearts while we were dealing with offenses and forgiveness? Because it is this love that heals the wounds of the heart—that is all the hurt that offenses imprint on our hearts—and it is from this healed heart that forgiveness flows. When your heart is filled with this love, all problems of life fade, including offenses you have suffered. The love of God makes you secure. When you know that the God who created the universe loves you, you understand that there is nothing for you to worry about if your life is in His hands. When you have trusted Him with your life, you also understand that nothing happens to you (and this includes offenses) that He is not aware of and that He has not allowed. And even if it was not His original plan, He still has a purpose for why it happened, and in the end, He will make all things work together for good to those who love Him (Romans 8:28). The love of God is liberating. It brings peace in the midst of chaos. It transcends human emotions. There is serenity and confidence in God as we navigate life with all the trials and troubles that come with it.

The love of God is binding. Nothing and no one can separate us from it (Romans 8), but we can walk away from it. I think of the nation of Israel on whom God had poured His love, but they walked away from it to serve and worship other gods to the point that they became strangers to God's love. At some point, God speaks to the nation through the prophet Malachi, saying, "I have loved you", and the people's reaction to God's statement is, "In what way have you loved us?" (Malachi 1:2). This is where it becomes important for us as disciples of Jesus Christ to understand Jesus's command in John 15:9, " ... abide in my love." We have talked about receiving God's forgiveness. We must also receive God's love and abide in it.

20 A HEART OF FORGIVENESS

Having received God's forgiveness and love, we must also cultivate a heart of forgiveness, a heart that is ready to forgive. We are all familiar with the conversation between Peter and Jesus. In Matthew 18:21, Peter asks Jesus, "How often shall my brother sin against me, and I forgive him? Up to seven times?" Jesus's reply must certainly have surprised Peter, for He told him, "Not up to seven times, but up to seventy times seven." And Peter thought he was being gracious by extending forgiveness up to seven times. One might ask the question, "What would Peter do if there was an offense from his brother after the seventh forgiveness?" This would probably result in a severed relationship. If you think this is exaggerated, just look at how many family relationships are broken today around you, and that probably includes your own family.

There is an implicit notion of time in Peter's question and in Jesus's reply. Whatever time frame Peter had in mind for his question, we can fairly assume that Jesus understood Peter's question and answered with that same time frame in mind. Because Peter doesn't explicitly mention a time frame in his question, we can suppose that he implied a lifetime. In that case, the question would read, "How often in a lifetime?" Of course, it is hard to imagine Peter extending forgiveness to his brother only seven times in a lifetime. I lean more towards a shorter time frame: How often in a day? The reason I think he meant a shorter time frame is because I have siblings, and I am raising children. I see how they interact on a daily basis. Most of the time, they behave like they cannot live together, and they cannot live apart from each other, either. It is a mystery to me. One minute, they are best buddies, and the next, they are mad at each other. Some days, this can happen many times. So, I can understand if Peter's time frame is a day. I also believe that Peter is thinking about a literal brother, because we tend to avoid any stranger or neighbor that offends us even once.

If it is the case that we are talking about multiple offenses coming from a close relationship, then let us examine Jesus's response to Peter. Peter had been gracious and patient enough to extend forgiveness seven times in a day. Let us agree that most of us would not. We would rather go to bed angry at the brother and carry on being angry for days. But Jesus is telling Peter that his patience and grace are not enough. Seven times is too little. Jesus raises the bar that was already too high for Peter, from seven to seventy times seven. I can imagine Peter's shock. Keep in mind that we are hypothetically talking about 490 times in a day that the same individual offends you and you forgive. That can only come from a close relationship. Today, a typical day in Israel is 12 hours, starting at 6 a.m. and ending at 6 p.m. If you do the math, you come down to an average of about forgiving the same offending individual every 1.5 minutes (1.469 to be precise). We are assuming that that individual is not offending you at night while he or she is sleeping, and you are also taking a break from their pestering. But Jesus is asking Peter to forgive every 1.5 minutes, basically to forgive constantly, to be permanently in a state of forgiving. I call this having a heart of forgiveness.

We established earlier that forgiveness flows from love. So, to have a heart of forgiveness also means that our hearts are constantly filled with love—not our own, but the love of God that we have just talked about. It is only the love of God in your heart that can change you into a patient, gracious, and forgiving person. Once that transformation happens in an individual, their life begins to give glory to God. That is when we can follow Paul's exhortation to forgive one another, even as God in Christ forgave us (Ephesians 4:32).

God Himself had instituted forgiveness as part of the cultural fabric of Israel, not only on the worship side, but also in the commandments. The Israelites were commanded to forgive debts (another word for offenses) every seven years and every 49 years. The forgiveness that happened in the 49th or 50th year was to be complete; no wonder it was called the year of favor. Likewise, God wants forgiveness to be ingrained in us, and we have several examples in the Bible of individuals who were deeply offended and chose the path of forgiveness.

David

We discussed the unforgiveness of King Saul that drove him to try to kill David on numerous occasions. It is not only that he cast the spear at David more than once intending to "pin David to the wall" (1 Samuel 18:11, 19:10), he also sent soldiers to kill David in his own home or bring him to Saul so he might kill him himself (1 Samuel 19:11-15), and he led the army of Israel on at least two expeditions with the only goal being to find and kill David (1 Samuel 24:1-2, 26:1-2).

Although not explicitly stated in the Bible, we can infer that David's attitude towards Saul was one of forgiveness. David did not even once try to retaliate or avenge himself. We know that David was a valiant man of war. On some occasions, David chose to escape instead of fighting back. On other occasions, he actually had the opportunity to kill Saul, but he chose to spare him, surrendering his case to God's sovereignty. When King Saul eventually dies, we don't see David rejoicing and celebrating; we see him grieving and mourning. David did not try to destroy Saul's family after Saul's death, as was customary when kingdoms changed hands. The war that went on between Saul's house and David's was instigated by people like Abner, Saul's uncle and the general of Saul's army, who thought that they could re-establish Saul's kingdom to his sons, even though they knew that God had chosen David to be the next king. Finally, we see David desiring to do good and show the kindness of God to Saul's descendants (2 Samuel 9). Only a forgiving heart can drive a person to behave like this.

Joseph

Joseph was a handsome young man who was hated by his brothers for being their father's favorite. Jacob, the father, did not even try to conceal the favoritism. He made a princely coat for Joseph, and that birthed jealousy in the siblings' hearts. To make matters worse, God gave Joseph dreams of one day being a ruler to whom the siblings would bow. Jealousy and hatred led the siblings to conspire to kill Joseph, but one of the siblings said killing him would not profit them, so they sold him as a slave, instead. Joseph was sold three times: first by his brothers to a caravan of Ishmaelites (distant cousins), then the Ishmaelites sold him to Midianites (other distant cousins), and finally the Midianites sold him in Egypt to Potiphar, the captain of Pharaoh's guard. You can read the story in Genesis 37. Joseph will find himself in prison for a crime he did not commit. Through all these miseries and troubles, the Bible tells us that "The Lord was with Joseph" (Genesis 39:2).

Eventually, Joseph would rise to power and become the second in command in Egypt (basically, the head of the executive branch), one of, if not the most, prosperous and powerful nations on earth at that time. Joseph's brothers were forced to go to Egypt to buy food for their families because of a severe drought throughout the region, for food was found only in Egypt thanks to God's wisdom through Joseph and God's forewarning through Pharaoh's dreams that only Joseph could interpret. The brothers unknowingly bowed to Joseph. But most importantly for us, Joseph forgave them, because he understood the events from God's perspective. Everything that had happened to him was actually pushing him closer to his godly destiny, to the fulfillment of God's plan for his life.

See, it is not only that God was with him. Joseph also nurtured a relationship with God by keeping himself away from sin and resisting temptation, even if he had to flee. In short, Joseph lived in the presence of God. Without God's perspective, which is only available in God's presence, the natural inclination of every human being that has suffered at the hands of other human beings is revenge, especially when one has all the power and means to exert it. What a great example of forgiveness we have in Joseph!

Stephen

Our third example comes from Stephen in Acts 6 and 7. The Bible does not tell us much about Stephen, but we know that he was a man of good reputation among the believers and disciples, full of the Holy Spirit and wisdom. He was chosen to be one of the seven deacons who helped with the practical things in the early church so that the apostles could focus on prayer and the ministry of the word of God. After these seven men were chosen, the apostles laid hands on them. This is significant, because right after the laying on of hands, the Bible tells us in Acts 6:8, "Stephen, full of faith and power, did great wonders and signs among the people." He was also a great orator and debater, because the people disputing with him could not resist the wisdom and spirit in him.

This Stephen was falsely accused of blasphemy (sounds familiar?). He was seized and dragged before a hostile council. We are not far removed in time from Jesus's death, so some members of this council may have been there when the same council condemned Jesus. His accusers stirred up the crowd and brought false witnesses against him. This is exactly what happened with Jesus's trial. But I want to draw your attention to Stephen's attitude and composure. While the crowd is raging, the false witnesses are spewing their lies, and the hostile council has most certainly condemned him to death in their hearts (except that by law they had to give him an opportunity to defend himself), the Bible says that those looking at him saw his face shining as the face of an angel. Wait a second—we have seen this before in the Bible. When Moses spent time in the presence of God, his face was glowing with God's glory (Exodus 34:29–35). You cannot spend time in God's presence and remain the same. It is impossible. Being in the presence of God always changes a person for the better, according to God's standards, of course. The same principle is at play here.

While people are busy mocking and falsely accusing, and others are still waiting to condemn him to death, before he even speaks a word for his own defense, Stephen is positioning his spirit, mind, and soul in the presence of God. He is communing with God. He is so much into God's presence that not only is his face shining in the presence of threats and false accusations, but the Holy Spirit actually uploads into Stephen's spirit the very words to speak, echoing what Jesus had told the disciples in Mark 13:11. All the time that Stephen is being seized, dragged before the council, falsely accused of blasphemy, judged unfairly, sentenced to death, and finally stoned to death, his spirit, mind, and soul are in the presence of God. He is receiving revelations and visions from God. There is no wonder that his last words, directed to God, were to forgive his accusers and everyone involved in the series of events that led to his stoning. Most of us would have been busy denying the accusations and vehemently defending ourselves with the proof of our innocence. He did no such things. He entered into God's presence and handled everything the way the Holy Spirit was directing him, including the forgiveness of his persecutors and murderers.

Entering the presence of God is not accidental, and it is not God's initiative. It is intentional of us. Stephen purposely entered into God's presence, and one of the results of his being in God's presence was that he forgave those stoning him. I don't know where, from whom, or how Stephen learned this very thing we saw in Jesus. As Jesus hung on the cross and was about to die, his eyes were open to see the world and its needs. His body was in indescribable pain, but His spirit and soul were in communion with the Father. Yes, Jesus was talking to the Father in the midst of his trial and pain, looking at things from God's perspective. His last words were directed to God. May we learn from such godly examples.

The Father of the Prodigal Son

Another New Testament example of forgiveness is in the parable of the prodigal son that Jesus told in Luke 15:11–32. He talks of a father who had two sons. The father was probably wealthy by local standards, because we are told that he had servants. One day, the younger son asks his father to give him his portion of the inheritance. This was a very unusual request from any son or daughter to a father. I am sure the father was shocked. A child didn't receive an inheritance until after the death of the parent who bequeathed his goods to his descendants or posterity. This younger son was actually wishing for the death of his father, and that the estate was already divided. We do not know how old this younger son was, but he must have been old enough to live by himself.

Here we have a young man who has been reared, loved, cherished, educated, and provided for by his father every day of his life since he was born, and who is enjoying all the benefits of living in his father's house. He now rises up and screams to his father's face, "I wish you were dead!!" Is there a worse betrayal than this? What father, in his right mind, would then grant the request of this ungrateful and unappreciative son? Whether grudgingly, reluctantly, or just willingly, we do know that eventually the father grants the son's request. The son leaves the father's house with his new wealth in his pocket and squanders it all on prodigal living. He eventually becomes homeless, jobless, and hungry, with nobody to care for him. The only job that he could find was guarding pigs, and he became so hungry and desperate that he desired to eat what the pigs were eating. It was at this lowest point in his life that he remembers that even the servants back in his father's house had enough to eat, and there he was, dying of hunger. He thus decides to go back home for the food, and while he was at it, he would also confess his sin to his father.

The young man makes the hard but good decision to go home to his father and confess his sin, with the hope of being hired on his father's farm as a way to earn his daily bread. The Bible says that while the young man "was still a great way off," the father saw him, recognized him, ran to him, and hugged and kissed his betraying and pig-smelling son, who had wished his death a few years earlier. There is no better image or portrayal of forgiveness than this father hugging and kissing his betraying son, before the son even opens his mouth to confess his sin. Such forgiveness is only found in the heart and love of God, the one that overlooks offenses as if they never happened, and restores broken relationships. Notice that after all of that, the father still calls him "my son" (Luke 15:24).

21 PARTAKERS OF THE DIVINE NATURE

Allow me to say here that offenses are not about the offender; they are about what God is doing in your life, developing His divine nature in you, forming Christ in you. The apostle Paul wrote to the disciples in Galatia, "My little children, for whom I labor in birth again until Christ is formed in you," Galatians 4:19. There were no doubts in Paul's mind that Christian living is about reflecting and emulating the life of Christ. In fact, the concept of discipleship implies two notions: one is the well-known notion of student, i.e., a student of a famous teacher. But discipleship also implies the less explored notion of emulating the lifestyle of the teacher, that is, a disciple not only learning from a teacher but also applying those things he or she is learning in order to arrive at the same lifestyle as the teacher.

We find this at play in Antioch (Acts 11:26), where and when the disciples of Jesus are first called "Christians," i.e., "of Christ," or "little Christs." In other words, the people around the disciples observed that their lives reflected Jesus's. This is what the apostle Paul is striving to drive the Galatian disciples towards. Christ has to be formed in the true disciple of Jesus. Actually, that is the only true mark of a believer in Jesus Christ. Anything else is just a profession of faith that lacks substance.

In 2 Peter 1:3, the apostle Peter tells us that God's divine power has given us all things that pertain to life and godliness, through the knowledge of Him who called us by glory and virtue. He goes on in verse 4 to say that by this glory and virtue, we have also been given exceedingly great and precious promises. Peter tells us that the purpose or reason why we have been given these promises is that we may be partakers of the divine nature. It is clear that the only divinity Peter is referring to is God the Father. I understand these verses to mean that God wants His nature to be in us and displayed to all around us. That divine nature includes love (God is love), from which forgiveness flows. Is that divine nature in you? Do people around you see Christ in you? Is God imprinting His nature in you? Are you allowing Him to do it?

How does God see that in us or help us understand that? He allows us to be in situations that require a demonstration of God's character and nature. When it comes to forgiveness, no other situation will require God's nature more than offenses. In other words, God will allow offenses to come into your life in order to show or display His divine nature in you. He allowed Jesus to be rejected, betrayed, falsely accused, lied about, beaten, mocked, and condemned. Remember that Jesus himself learned obedience through the things that He suffered (Hebrews 5:8). He allowed Stephen to go through the same circumstances. He allowed Joseph to be betrayed, sold as a slave, falsely accused, and thrown in jail. He allowed the apostles to be beaten, falsely accused, and thrown in jail. In all these examples, the outcome from the offended was forgiveness. The apostle Peter tells us, "The same sufferings are experienced by the brotherhood in the world" (1 Peter 5:9). How does Peter say we should respond to the suffering inflicted on us?

If we accept the premise that God is imprinting His divine nature and character in us, and as believers there should not even be an "if", then we must also accept that the various offenses we suffer are regular evaluations from God to see where we are in this journey of being transformed into the image of His Son. Thus, we must understand that offenses are tools in God's hands for perfecting us. We must take our eyes and emotions off the offenders, as it is no longer about the offenders; it is all about what God is doing in our lives. This is what Joseph and Stephen did.

There is another aspect of this thought that we must also consider. Remember, the offenses we suffer are wounds of the heart that are only healed in God's presence by the outpouring of His love. Seeking this healing outside of God's love and presence is worthless and futile. However, seeking God's love and presence draws us closer to God, which is the very desire of God and should be the goal of every believer. Thus, God is not just using offenses to perfect us; He is also using them, along with other trials of life, to draw us closer to Himself. I know that by nature we don't like offenses, and I am not advocating that we like them. I don't wish offenses on anyone, for I know the damage they can cause. But I have also come to know that offenses are tools in God's hands for perfecting us and drawing us closer to Himself. From this standpoint, I will no longer look at or react to offenses in the same way.

22 MY MOTHER'S HOUSE

Several years ago, my mother was diagnosed with Alzheimer's disease. We had noticed before the diagnosis that she was having memory lapses, but we were not aware of the severity or the rapid degradation. At the time of the diagnosis, she was living with my sister in Europe, and the doctors recommended that she return to Cameroon to live in the environment where she had long-term memories. At that time, she had no home of her own to return to. My siblings and I were hustling to raise our families, and none of us had the means to build her a house. It had always been her desire and prayer that one day she would have a place she could call home, regardless of the materials used to build it. Even though there was no money saved in the bank to build her a house, I did own a second house as a rental property. This was the first house that my wife and I bought and lived in. It was damaged during Hurricane Katrina in 2005. We used the insurance money to pay it off, and we rebuilt it with the help of friends and volunteers. It is this house that my wife and I sold so we could build my mom a house in Cameroon.

My five siblings and I agreed to inform our uncles and aunts of the desire and plans to build our mom a house on our grandfather's compound, the place where she grew up, as she would be surrounded by familiar faces. The close family back in Cameroon sat in on a meeting, attended by my younger brother Christian (who at the time was the only sibling living in Cameroon), three aunts, an uncle, and our grandmother. Absent from the meeting was another uncle who lives overseas, but he had consented to the meeting. The purpose of the meeting was to designate the place where we would build the house for Mom. The meeting went well, at least as reported to us, and it was decided that my grandmother would show my brother Christian where to build the house.

When we drew the plans and the work of laying the foundation began, my two uncles and all the aunts, except for one, stood in opposition to the building project. Now these are the people that my mother, being the eldest of all of them, nurtured and cared for as her own children for many years. As a matter of fact, there was a time when my two youngest aunts and my two uncles lived in my mother's modest rented house. I witnessed my mom's sacrifices for her younger siblings, the same people who were now standing in opposition to building her a house on their father's compound at the time when she was vulnerable and could not even speak for herself.

Of all the offenses and betrayals that I have suffered in life, this one was the hardest and harshest. Yes, to this date, this one ranks as the deepest and most painful wound of the heart that I have ever suffered. I guess I loved my mom that profoundly, and so I could not endure seeing and witnessing injustice and hatred against her, especially at the time when she was not able to even speak coherently. I did not mind the fact that the only piece of land left on the compound where we were building her house was close to the swamp, but I could not tolerate such stabbing in the back of a defenseless and weak person. All of us, as her children, were stunned. For a long time, I was very angry and bitter towards both my uncles and the two aunts who had orchestrated this hatred. I could have understood if the motivation was that women did not inherit property by tradition, but a recent law in the country had brought that traditional law under the subjection of the laws of the republic, which stipulate that men and women equally inherit property from their parents. By the way, one of the aunts behind this conspiracy had already built a house for herself on a separate piece of property that the grandfather owned, and there was no family council that gathered to decide, let alone approve, her building project. Also, the youngest aunt was living in the house that the grandfather left. So, it was not just hatred; it was also injustice, which I really don't like from the bottom of my heart.

As time went on and the positions became entrenched, I became more and more bitter towards my uncles and aunts and retreated into resentment and bitterness. While all this was happening, I was serving God, as I have always done. No one around me could have imagined what I was going through. I may have shared this with only a few people. The bitterness and anger grew and began to dominate my thoughts. One day, I found myself on the verge of praying that God would do something bad to my uncles and aunts. And that's when the Spirit of God quickened my spirit. I remember having a conversation within myself, saying to myself, "I am a servant of God; I cannot pray such a prayer." That was the turning point for me, and I began to ask God to help me out of bitterness and anger, and most importantly, help me forgive, for I knew all too well what the Bible teaches about forgiveness.

I don't recall how much time had passed since then, but I do remember that one day I was in the presence of God, and the Spirit of God engaged me in a conversation. I don't know how God speaks to you as a reader; that is yours to find out and grow into. But I have come to know the difference between my thoughts, the devil's thoughts, and God's voice in my spirit, and I know this was God speaking to me. I remember this as if it happened yesterday. The Holy Spirit asked me the question, "The people who crucified Jesus, did they do it on purpose?" I answered, "Lord, how can someone crucify another by accident?" I mean, the crucifixion is a very intentional act, and besides, the Bible tells us the motives for crucifying Jesus. It was a well-premeditated, well-concocted, and well-executed plan from the leaders of the people, the ruling class, which consisted of highly educated men. I was very satisfied with my answer to God. Then came the second question from the Holy Spirit: How did Jesus pray for the very people that were crucifying

Him? We all know the answer to this question. The Holy Spirit did not stop there. He went on to say, "See, there are things that people do intentionally, with clear purpose, but when God looks at those very acts, He sees ignorance. They do not know what they are doing."

The crucifiers knew full well what they were doing, in all forms of human understanding of this physical world, yet Jesus said that they don't know what they do. Does that not remind you of, "My ways are not your ways," from Isaiah 55:8? Note that when it comes to the crucifixion, Jesus makes ignorance the basis of forgiveness (Luke 23:34). The same principle is at play when God forgives Nineveh. In Jonah 4:11, God asks the prophet, "And should I not pity Nineveh, that great city, in which are more than one hundred and twenty thousand persons who cannot discern between their right hand and their left—and much livestock?" It is my humble opinion that God saw the people of Nineveh as ignorant. How else would you describe a person who cannot discern his right from his left? I venture to say here that whatever our offenders did, they did it in ignorance, at least from God's perspective. If you question this basis, well, go back to the cross and ask Jesus to help you see things the way God sees them.

I decided that day that if God sees them as ignorant, so will I. And agreeing with God that the offenders acted in ignorance opened the door to forgiveness. The weight and pain of the betrayal lifted from my shoulders. The bitterness began to fade away, and I began to have peace on this matter.

23 IGNORANCE MUCH

But what is this ignorance? How do I get to know that they acted in ignorance? I think of Saul of Tarsus, who persecuted the church and oversaw the stoning of Stephen. He later came to Christ and became the apostle Paul. He tells us that all the violence perpetrated against the believers while he was persecuting the church was done ignorantly (1 Timothy 1:13). Peter tells us in Acts 3:17 that the people who crucified Jesus did it in ignorance. We must agree with God that the offenders are acting in ignorance. I am not excusing them or saying they are not responsible for what they did. Not at all! What I am trying to say in the next paragraph is that there is something else going on, from God, that the offenders are not aware of. In 1 Corinthians 2:6–8, the apostle Paul tells us, "If the rulers of this age had known the wisdom of God, they would not have crucified the Lord of Glory." Do you see the ignorance?

You must learn to see things the way God sees them, and He only occasionally lifts the veil from our eyes. I discussed earlier that this happens in the presence of God. However, there is another point that I want to stress here to help us see their ignorance. I am going to assume here that, as in Jesus's case, the offenders have taken the position of an enemy, and they were determined to harm and destroy you on purpose, just as the very definition of the word enemy implies. An enemy cannot and will not do anything that will turn out to be good or beneficial to you. They will not seek your promotion or welfare. They are only focused on destroying you.

Remember that God is wiser than men and can use men to fulfill His purpose. The following are five aspects or areas of their ignorance, and there may be more.

The Offenders Do Not Know: Part 1

They don't know that God will make their offenses work together for good to you.

In Romans 8:28, the apostle Paul teaches us, "All things work together for good to those who love God, to those who are called according to His purposes." It is my hope and prayer that you are one of those the apostle is referring to, someone who loves God and who is called according to His purposes. But I want to draw your attention to the person who is writing this verse. By the time Paul writes this epistle, he has already gone through quite some tribulations and persecutions, and at least one of these leaves him almost dead. He writes that at some point he came close to despairing. Yet, it is this person who tells us that all these things worked together for good for him. In other words, he came to see the good that God intended through all these things. I consider Romans 8:28 to be a personal testament from Paul, just as he also tells us in verse 37 of the same chapter, writing, "In all these things we are more than conquerors through Him who loved us." The list of things over which we are more than conquerors is given in verse 35, and it includes tribulation, distress, persecution, nakedness, and the sword. I omitted famine because I think it is outside of human control. But all the other "things" on this list were inflicted on Paul and his companions by enemies, and we would rightfully be offended if anyone inflicted such things on us. However, Paul says that these worked together for good to him. If God made these things work together for good to Paul and his friends, the same God, who has not changed since then, will also make our tribulations and offenses work together for good to us.

The Offenders Do Not Know: Part 2

They don't know what God is doing or planning to do in your life, and whatever God is doing or has planned for you and me is ultimately good.

To be honest, offenses catch us off guard because we are not aware of what God is doing in our lives at the moment they happen. If we ourselves are not aware of what God is doing in us at the moment, how much less are the offenders aware? The Bible tells us in Micah 4:12, "But they do not know the thoughts of the LORD, nor do they understand His counsel ..." God is always up to something in our lives. Nothing happens to us that catches Him by surprise—nothing that He did not allow, approve, or ordain. In any case, He always has a purpose for everything that He does or allows. In Isaiah 55, God flatly says, "My thoughts are not your thoughts." See, the thoughts of the offenders are to do you harm (think of Joseph's brothers), but those are not God's thoughts. You want to know God's thoughts? Read Jeremiah 29:11, a verse that is being spoken to people living under oppression and captivity in the land of their enemies. If God had good thoughts towards them in the midst of their oppression and captivity, the same God, who has not changed since then, also has good thoughts towards you as you go through the pain of offenses. And what are those thoughts? To prosper you, to give you a future and hope, and basically to bless and restore you, with confidence to boot. Do the offenders have any hint of that? I don't think so. Again, I take Joseph's brothers as an example. They had no clue whatsoever about what God was thinking toward Joseph at the time they were selling him as a slave out of jealousy, envy, and hatred. But we know how the story went.

The Offenders Do Not Know: Part 3

God's wisdom at its finest: they do not know that they are helping you fulfill the plan and mission of God for your life.

As a child and servant of God, there is nothing that you and I should desire more than fulfilling God's plans and purpose for our lives. In Jesus's example, God's plan included the cross. Think of it: what offense can be worse than being betrayed by a close friend, abandoned by almost everyone, and ending up on a cross—the most painful and shameful death at the time? Betrayal alone is already bad as an offense. Add to it being abandoned by your closest friends at the time you are betrayed, seized for a crime you did not commit, and finally, sentenced to death on the cross in a mockery of a trial that was driven by envy, jealousy, and hatred. The Jewish council sentenced Jesus to death for claiming that He was the Son of God, the Messiah. But they were actually helping Him fulfill the prophecies about the Messiah; that is, their very actions were fulfilling what was to be done to the Messiah. On one hand, they were denying Him the Messiahship, and on the other hand, they were raising Him to the Messiahood through a death sentence that was supposed to end any aspiration of being a Messiah, should He have had such. Do you see the ignorance and blindness here?

Jesus actually had the opportunity and means to protect and defend Himself, and even strike down those arresting him. However, He relinquished that right to submit to the Father's will in fulfilling the Scriptures. We read in Matthew 26:54–56, "[54] How then could the Scriptures be fulfilled, that it must happen thus?" [55] In that hour Jesus said to the multitudes, "Have you come out, as against a robber, with swords and clubs to take Me? I sat daily with you, teaching in the temple, and you did not seize Me. [56] But all this was done that the Scriptures of the prophets might be fulfilled." Jesus understood and lived all His life in fulfillment of the Scriptures. He had said earlier in Matthew 26:24, "The Son of

Man indeed goes just as it is written of Him, …" which is also echoed in Mark 14:21 and Luke 22:22.

Jesus had enemies; He knew that He would be betrayed—why, when, and by whom—yet, He never called any of the people involved in the planning of His destruction enemies, nor did He refer to them as such. He is the one who taught us to love our enemies. Even at the very moment He was being betrayed and arrested, He was calling Judas Iscariot "friend." I want to say here that although we have been offended and hurt by many people, unfortunately, and although there are people out there who actively seek to hurt and harm us, unfortunately, you and I do not have enemies. No, we don't. We do not fight against flesh and blood (Ephesians 6). We are surrounded by a bunch of people who have been blinded and deceived by the real enemy, the devil, and who are also ignorant. We should not fall into the same trap of blindness. What do I mean? We should not place people's evil actions above God's sovereignty. Jesus was fully aware that all these bad actors were actually executing God's plan—the things He had foreordained. Peter says in Acts 2:23, "Him, being delivered by the determined purpose and foreknowledge of God, you have taken by lawless hands, have crucified, and put to death." Then in Acts 3:17–18, we read, "Yet now, brethren, I know that you did it in ignorance, as did also your rulers. But those things which God foretold by the mouth of all His prophets, that the Christ would suffer, He has thus fulfilled."

It is also how the disciples understood it as they prayed in Acts 4:27–28, saying, "For truly against Your holy Servant Jesus, whom You anointed, both Herod and Pontius Pilate, with the Gentiles and the people of Israel, were gathered together to do whatever Your hand and Your purpose determined before to be done." Finally, in Acts 13:26–29, we read:

> "[26] Men and brethren, sons of the family of Abraham, and those among you who fear God, to you the word of this salvation has been sent. [27] For those who dwell in Jerusalem,

and their rulers, because they did not know Him, nor even the voices of the Prophets which are read every Sabbath, have fulfilled them in condemning Him. [28] And though they found no cause for death in Him, they asked Pilate that He should be put to death. [29] Now when they had fulfilled all that was written concerning Him, they took Him down from the tree and laid Him in a tomb."

Most of us do not have the vantage point of Jesus, the privilege of knowing beforehand the plans of God for our lives. We do not have prophecies that foretell our life mission, and that certainly contributes to how we react to offenses, because we don't immediately see how the offenses line up with the will of God for our lives.

The same scenario happened with Joseph. The brothers sold him as a slave to put an end to the dreams of leadership that he had dreamt of, yet, their actions actually drove him closer to the fulfillment of those dreams. Imagine being a brother to Joseph, who conspired and approved that he be sold as a slave. How ignorant would you appear when you hear from Joseph's lips, "It was not you who sent me here, but God" (Genesis 45:8)? The other administrators that were jealous of Daniel and tried to destroy him in order to prevent him from being promoted by the emperor found out the hard way that their plan actually ended up handing him the very promotion they tried so hard to keep him away from. On the surface, it appears that the offenders are succeeding, but being unaware of God's plans and purposes in His infinite and manifold wisdom, they do not know that God is actually using their actions to get us closer and closer to fulfilling His plans and purposes for our lives. The problem is that we get caught up in the flesh, looking at the offenses and offenders from human understanding, because we ourselves do not know what God's plan is for our lives. But when it happened to him, Jesus knew! We can also know, by developing a close relationship with God and dwelling in His presence. That's where God's plans are revealed.

The Offenders Do Not Know: Part 4

God is moving you from sensitivity to maturity.

Some of us are, or used to be, too sensitive in certain areas of our lives, and we would be offended anytime someone touched any of those areas. Some people also get offended at offenses that are not theirs, like when you get offended at the person who did not offend you but offended your friend. Some other people get offended by any misunderstanding. Finally, there are numerous cases where people get offended by the same thing over and over again. I used these examples because they have a common root: emotional immaturity. The truth is that as we grow in different areas of life, we must also grow in our emotions.

We must grow in understanding, wisdom, and discernment when it comes to offenses. We must analyze why we get offended by certain circumstances, words, or attitudes (the triggers), and learn to avoid or shelter our soul from them. This is how we learn not to be easily offended (1 Corinthians 13:5). We must also learn from past offenses and how to handle new ones. Ultimately, we must arrive at being offended only by the things that offend God; that is, we must learn to even ignore some offenses and just move on, because they are not worth the time and emotional energy spent on them. God will allow all types of potential offenses to hit you, because the way you handle them determines how you are growing emotionally. Why does that matter to God? Your emotional maturity is tied to your character, and it will show up in the way you act and react. Both your actions and reactions are supposed to reflect the divine nature and character that God is developing in you. See, the offenders do not know that they are helping you mature as a believer by learning not to be easily offended and how to handle future offenses. This is what God is busy doing in your life. God has blinded your offenders in ignorance for your sake. I pray God will open your eyes to see that it is not about the offenders anymore.

Of course, the offenses reveal the hearts and intentions of the offenders, but that is what everyone can see and understand. The believer must ask the more important questions: Why did God allow this in my life at this time? How am I supposed to handle this? Is there something to learn from this? Lord, what are you teaching me, or how are you developing me through this? As you ask the questions, be confident that God will answer them, and be aware that He may not answer immediately. Seeking God to answer these questions is more important than telling everyone and complaining about how bad the offense and the offender are.

This is not to say that we should not share our pain with other trusted friends and believers. We should, but we must dig deeper. This process of seeking God, by itself, actually produces spiritual growth in you when it is sustained. Any tree can grow roots in times of rain because of the available water. But only the strong trees can continue to grow roots and survive in the drought because their root systems want to reach the aquifer, however deep it may be. Those are the trees that you see in the ruthless deserts. Are your spiritual and emotional roots seasonal or permanent?

The Offenders Do Not Know: Part 5

Your pain puts you in the position to help others.

As you grow from the offenses, you gain understanding that will help other people and other believers heal from offenses. Here we see that the offenses, and by extension the offenders, are not only helping to make you a stronger believer, but they are also now helping you become more effective in ministry, thus helping to build the kingdom of God. The offenders have absolutely no clue about this. Again, this is God's wisdom at work, and I speak from experience. I wrote earlier about what I consider to be the worst and most painful offense I have ever endured. As much as this book is helping and will help people to deal with unforgiveness or to understand forgiveness, all that I write stems from what I learned through those offenses. I cannot deny the reality of the pain I went through and the wickedness of the offenders, but I can confidently look back today and see what God was doing, or at least what He was preparing. I have never had the desire to write a book. I don't consider myself a writer, much less a skilled one. If someone would have told me that I would one day write a book, I would have just scoffed at the idea. This was never on my agenda or in my dreams. Yet, I have witnessed the power and the hand of God at work every time I've shared my experiences or the lessons learned in the process.

Jesus said in John 12:24, "Most assuredly, I say to you, unless a grain of wheat falls into the ground and dies, it remains alone; but if it dies, it produces much grain." You would think that the death of the grain was the end of its life and story, however, That's not what Jesus is saying in this verse. On the contrary, there is exponentially more life coming out of the dying grain, meaning there is more to enjoy, more to celebrate, and more to give thanks for from the dying grain.

Most of us don't like the idea of dying in the flesh, so if God told us in advance what He has in mind, that He wants us to die in the flesh so that others may live, we would try to find our way out of it. Only Jesus could handle it and be obedient to the end. God does not tell us; He just lets the offenses catch us by surprise. But He will also let us go through the pain of offenses under His watchful eye and caring hand. The point is that there is life for others in your dying in the flesh. The majority of people who enjoy olive oil and its many benefits are oblivious to the painful process that the olives go through. Imagine being a harvested, ripe olive left to dry in the hot sun for days and then crushed under heavy stones. Even diamonds come from subjecting carbon to high pressure and temperature for a long time. If you struggle with the idea that your pain and suffering from offenses can be used by God for someone else's benefit, then you are actually struggling with the very foundation of Christianity and how God operates. Remember that Jesus was crushed in Gethsemane for our salvation. God may allow you to be crushed by offenses so that someone else may benefit from your crushing. This is where God redeems your story and owns it. It becomes His story, and He begins to use it for His glory. It is so wonderful to witness that it fills your soul with praises to God and unending Hallelujahs. This is what we usually pray for, for God to be glorified in our lives, being oblivious or ignorant as to how He might actually do it.

24 FROM THE MISSION FIELD

Sierra Leone

I remember being tasked with teaching a session on conflict resolution at a pastor's conference during a mission trip to Sierra Leone. We organized pastors' conferences in several places during any given trip. On this particular trip, we had planned two conferences, one in Waterloo and one in Gbendembu. The Waterloo conference came first, and I taught my session out of the material I had prepared. It went so well that everyone was asking for my notes after the session. I intended to teach out of the same material at the pastors conference in Gbendembu, which was three days later. One day before teaching my session in Gbendembu, I began sensing in my spirit that God was leading me not to teach from my notes on the topic, but rather to share what I had learned about forgiveness. I wrestled with the thought all that day and night but resolved to follow God in whatever direction He was leading me. When I took the microphone to teach my session, I told all the pastors and church leaders gathered that I had prepared notes to teach from, but I was now going to share a personal testimony in obedience to the Holy Spirit. So, I told them the story of my mother's house that I summarized earlier in this book, the hatred, jealousy, and betrayal from her siblings, my anger, disappointment, and bitterness towards them, and how God led me to forgiveness and peace. I closed the session with a call to forgiveness and prayer.

When we broke for lunch, Pastor Daniel Kanu, the local organizer and coordinator of the pastors conference in Gbendembu, came to me with excitement on his face, telling me that the testimony was powerful. With a little doubt in my heart, I asked him, "How do you know?" I wish I could convey the joy and excitement from Pastor Daniel, but those things are lived in the moment; you just have to be there and see. He went on to say that one person in the audience came to see him to repent and confess their intention and plans for exacting vengeance. This pastor had been attacked by someone who went as far as to use witchcraft to destroy his life. He was now planning to go destroy this enemy after attending the pastor's conference, but he changed his mind under God's conviction from the testimony I gave. I don't know how many people were changed by my testimony that day, but I know that, at least for this one pastor, the message was not in vain. He repented and decided to forgive. I can only praise God for that.

Burkina Faso

Another testimony came to me in February 2022 during a mission trip to Burkina Faso. I was invited by the serving president of the Mission Apostolique and all its leadership team to teach at their annual pastors conference. I was also scheduled to teach the students at their two Bible schools that were dedicated to training workers of the kingdom and the gathering of church elders, deacons, and other helpers.

I had traveled to Burkina Faso two years earlier with my good friend, Pastor Josué Gómez from Corvallis (Oregon), to minister there. It was a short two-day trip, a detour on our way to Sierra Leone. This time, though, the invitation was directed to me only, so I traveled alone. This was one of the best mission trips so far. As much as the pastors, elders, deacons, and Bible school students were blessed, I think I was even more blessed and transformed by the testimonies that followed.

Before I left for the trip, I had a meeting with my senior pastor, and I felt the Lord leading me to ask him the specific question, "Is there something you wish someone had told you before you became a pastor?" I was sensing that that question would come up at the pastors' conference during the trip. When I asked him the question, his answer was prompt and emphatic, as if he had anticipated and was waiting for the question and needed no thinking to respond. His answer was, "People will betray you." Quite frankly, I was taken aback for a split second, as that was definitely not the answer I expected. Nonetheless, I wrote it down and went on the trip.

I remember a session I was teaching to pastors about the heart of a minister. We explored several characteristics of the heart in ministry, like how to develop a good heart and how to turn away from the bad heart that manifests itself in grudges, bitterness, and unforgiveness. As I was teaching this particular session, I moved around the room filled with pastors, and, seemingly randomly (I cannot claim that I was led by the Holy Spirit), I put my hand on a pastor's shoulder while I was talking about betrayal and forgiveness. This very pastor came to give me his testimony from the conference as we sat in the office of the Mission Apostolique National President.

He began his testimony by thanking God for sending me to Burkina Faso, then continued:

> "We (the pastors who attended the conference) are very happy to have had you with us all this week. I am the sitting General Secretary on the Executive Board of the Mission Apostolique for all Burkina Faso. We are serving our second term in office. We have organized many seminars, but at this pastors' conference, we witnessed something special. We have seen how God used you and how God spoke through your person. Personally, I can testify that your mission trip to Burkina Faso this year was for me. In my life, I have suffered many injustices, so to speak, and this pastors'

conference came to put me back on the right path, because I had decided to do things a certain way, but God corrected me through the conference. Another testimony is that I have raised and groomed someone in ministry for 29 years. For all 29 years, I had all my trust and confidence in, and even invested my life in this person. I trusted him. I was even preparing to elevate him higher in ministry. But what I saw became a great disappointment. One day I was sending him to execute a mission, and he revealed to me that he had been building a church for the last three years without telling me a word and was ready to hold a dedication service. He did not even want me to know. That wounded me for the trust that I had in him and for all that I had invested in him. I started asking what it was that I had done to him, but he never gave an answer. I was very shocked. And in my heart, this was a very deep wound. And I have been struggling since then. This happened in 2020. And God used you not only to bring me back to the right path but also to heal my wound. Because I had decided never to trust a person again and never to fully invest myself in a person to help them grow and move forward. But through your teaching and your personal testimonies, I understood that I am not the only one that God puts to the test. And I understood that, despite being over 60 years old, God still wants to teach me how to grow and move forward. I give God the glory. And from this conference, my vision for my ministry changes, and my dedication, consecration, and commitment to God change for the better, in the positive direction, for the glory of God. I am grateful to God, and I am also thankful for your obedience to the voice of God, and I pray that God will protect you and your family, your ministry, your church and pastor, all the leaders, and anyone who contributed for you to come on this trip. May God bless them. May God always open doors for you, for His glory. May God give you a long life so that you will see with your eyes the fruit of all that you do. To God alone be glory; to God alone be glory; to God alone be glory, to God alone be glory, Amen. We'll see each other another time. Thank you very much. Thank you, thank you. Really, I am very, very happy. Really, when you touched my problem, that was also when your hand touched my shoulder."

Another pastor and wife testified that they had kept wounds of the heart too long, and now it was time for them to be healed by God. A woman said she felt like the film of her life in ministry was being played before her eyes—how she had suffered so many betrayals, and now God was relieving and restoring her. There were many more testimonies from pastors that same day about what they learned about forgiveness. I myself am still amazed at the memories and testimonies from this trip. These were people I had never seen or met before and may never see again.

I keep going back to watch some videos and just praise God for what he did with the little I had in my hand and heart. Since God has no favorites, whatever he did or does for me and through me, he can and will do for and through you also. Who would have thought that the lesson learned from my offenses would bring healing to other pastors established in ministry for over 30 and 40 years? I hope these testimonies are enough to show you that some olive oil came from my crushing and brought some life to others from my dying through offenses. God has redeemed the story of my offenses and is now using it for His own glory. I can only praise Him and count myself blessed and privileged at the same time. Yet, I am more than convinced that God wants to heal you from the wounds of your heart and redeem the story of your offenses, as well, for His glory and praise. The examples that I used in this book all follow this theme: from Joseph's crushing came life, hope and salvation from famine for many lives, and God healed him, and his story is still being used today as an example of forgiveness. That's what I am talking about. And who knows—maybe that is what offenses are all about? God will enlighten us all on that question.

Now that you understand their ignorance, how do you handle it? I have already mentioned that on the cross, Jesus prayed to the Father, asking Him to forgive his offenders whose actions were based on their ignorance. Another powerful statement that follows on this theme is found in Acts 17:30, "Truly, these times of ignorance God overlooked, but now commands all men everywhere to repent." Guess what God does for people who repent? He forgives and saves them, but the more important point here is that God overlooks ignorance. We must learn to overlook the ignorance of the offenders, as God's children and servants, but more importantly as people in whom God is imprinting His divine nature, as people in whom God has poured out His Spirit and love, and also as people who used to walk in ignorance.

25 PROVISION FOR IGNORANCE

In the book of Hebrews 9:6-7, we read that the high priest went into the most holy place to present the blood of the sacrifice for atonement of the sins that he himself and the people committed in ignorance. The writer of the book of Hebrews is echoing a provision that was first mentioned in Leviticus 5:17–18, where we read, "17If a person sins, and commits any of these things which are forbidden to be done by the commandments of the Lord, though he does not know it, yet he is guilty and shall bear his iniquity. 18 And he shall bring to the priest a ram without blemish from the flock, with your valuation, as a trespass offering. So the priest shall make atonement for him regarding his ignorance in which he erred and did not know it, and it shall be forgiven him." Here, God Himself is speaking and giving instructions to and through Moses. God is fully aware that the person has sinned by committing things that are forbidden in His commandments and is guilty, even though, by God's own assessment, the person did it in ignorance. God made provisions for the forgiveness of sins committed in ignorance. This is what we see in action when God forgives Nineveh, when Jesus is on the cross praying and asking God to forgive those who condemned Him.

I know that offenses differ in the level of pain they can inflict. They range from the frivolous (people just being offended by anything these days) to the more serious. It is not my job to rank where your offenses fall on this broad spectrum. I started with the premise that you cannot carry on with your unforgiveness to heaven, because God wants you to forgive, and He won't forgive you if you don't forgive. You cannot even carry the burden of your unforgiveness much longer in this lifetime. It is rotting and ruining your life. I have shared some of my own experiences and the lessons learned along the way, as well as how God has redeemed the story of my worst offense and is now using it for His own glory. I am forever thankful to God for the day He took the time to open my eyes and began to reveal Himself and speak to my soul on this painful and sensitive subject. It is my prayer and hope that God will do the same for you and through you. I hope to have made it clear that you cannot forgive on your own, from your wounded heart and emotions. You need God! And the good news is that you can find Him. He is willing and ready to welcome you in His presence, where you will find healing for your heart, soul, and mind through His love. He will also open your eyes to show you what He was busy doing, along with the ignorance of your offenders. When you begin to see the offenders as ignorant and lost, you also begin to have compassion for them and plead God's mercy over their lives, if God's character has begun to take root in your soul. Then you will also have the same desires for them as God Himself has, which is their salvation. And now that you understand their ignorance, it is my prayer that you will deal with their ignorance the same way God Himself dealt with yours. Remember that you were also ignorant when you walked in sin (Ephesians 4:17–19, Hebrews 9:7, 1 Peter 1:14), but God overlooked your ignorance (Acts 17:30) and drew you to Jesus unto salvation. Jesus said in John 6:44, "No one can come to Me unless the Father who sent Me draws him; and I will raise him up at the last day." As God is busy developing His divine nature in you, I pray you will get to the point where you overlook the ignorance of your offenders and pray for their salvation. That is the mark of a heart that has been healed from the poison of unforgiveness.

I will close this book with a poignant story that you may have heard about, because it summarizes all the principles we've explored. For helping, hiding, and smuggling Jews out of the Nazi persecution, Corrie Ten Boom and her sister Betsie were arrested by the Nazis and sent to a concentration camp. Many of us have heard of and read about the horrors of the Nazi concentration camps. Corrie witnessed her sister Betsie die in pain in the concentration camp. Corrie was a devout Christian who led worship in the concentration camp. She was miraculously released on a clerical error and became a renowned evangelist who often preached on love and forgiveness. A former Nazi guard in the concentration camp where she witnessed her sister Betsie dying came to her after she finished preaching in a church service, and she was confronted with the difficulty of forgiving. These are her own words describing the experience, exerted from her book titled *The Hiding Place*:

> It was at a church service in Munich that I saw him, a former S.S. man who had stood guard at the shower room door in the processing center at Ravensbruck. He was the first of our actual jailers that I had seen since that time. And suddenly it was all there – the roomful of mocking men, the heaps of clothing, Betsie's pain-blanched face.
>
> He came up to me as the church was emptying, beaming and bowing. "How grateful I am for your message, Fraulein." He said. "To think that, as you say, He has washed my sins away!" His hand
>
> was thrust out to shake mine. And I, who had preached so often to the people in Bloemendaal the need to forgive, kept my hand at my side.
>
> Even as the angry, vengeful thoughts boiled through me, I saw the sin of them. Jesus Christ had died for this man; was I going to ask for more? Lord Jesus, I prayed, forgive me and help me to forgive him. I tried to smile, I struggled to raise my hand. I could not. I felt nothing, not the slightest spark of warmth or charity. And so again I breathed a

silent prayer. Jesus, I prayed, I cannot forgive him. Give me Your forgiveness.

As I took his hand the most incredible thing happened. From my shoulder along my arm and through my hand a current seemed to pass from me to him, while into my heart sprang a love for this stranger that almost overwhelmed me. And so I discovered that it is not on our forgiveness any more than on our goodness that the world's healing hinges, but on His. When He tells us to love our enemies, He gives, along with the command, the love itself (Ten Boom, 1971).

26 STARK WARNINGS

We have discussed the dangers and damages that unforgiveness generates in the lives of the offended and the people around them, and how far and how long that can endure. We have also discussed the process of reaching or achieving forgiveness. Yet, to those who deem that their offenses are too great to forgive, I want to remind them of the stark warnings that Jesus gave to His disciples on two occasions in the gospel of Matthew. First, in Matthew 6:14–15, right after teaching the model prayer to the disciples, He said, "¹⁴For if you forgive men their trespasses, your heavenly Father will also forgive you. ¹⁵ But if you do not forgive men their trespasses, neither will your Father forgive your trespasses." Notice that the model prayer includes a plea to be forgiven by God, but that plea itself is equated to our own forgiveness. Matthew 6:12 says it well, "And forgive us our debts, as we forgive our debtors." Now we are all aware that no one is without sin. That means we all need God's forgiveness. When we fail to forgive our offenders, we begin to live under guilt and condemnation. But that's not all.

In Matthew 18:21–35, Jesus tells the story of the unforgiving servant and concludes it with a serious warning that we must all take to heart. We talked about the unforgiving servant earlier when we discussed the ratio of debts, from the perspective that we are the ones who owed God the greater debt because of our sins. This servant fails to forgive his fellow servant, who owes him only 100 denarii. Notice the treatment that he receives in the end, as told by

Jesus Himself: "³²Then his master, after he had called him, said to him, 'You wicked servant! I forgave you all that debt because you begged me. ³³Should you not also have had compassion on your fellow servant, just as I had pity on you?' ³⁴And his master was angry, and delivered him to the torturers until he should pay all that was due to him. ³⁵So My heavenly Father also will do to you if each of you, from his heart, does not forgive his brother his trespasses."

Jesus is saying that what happened to this wicked servant is also what God the Father Himself will do to those who choose not to forgive their offenders. It is not just that the Father will not forgive those who don't forgive, He will also subject them to a harsh and bitter punishment at the hands of torturers. There are three important things to point out in verse 34: the master's anger, the punishment, and the duration of this punishment. Depending on the Bible translation, the unforgiving servant is thrown in jail to be tortured, or just handed to torturers. The word "torturers" in verse 34 can also be translated as "tormentors." The duration of the punishment is not specified; it is tied to the amount of debt, which is enormous in the case of this wicked servant. We can safely assume that it was going to be a long time. Finally, the wicked servant was handed to the torturers out of his master's anger.

Jesus then concludes this teaching to His disciples by telling them in verse 35 that this is what the Father "will do to you if each of you does not forgive ..." It seems plausible to infer that the combination of the anger of God the Father and a lengthy punishment under torturers or torments refers to the eternal punishment in hell. I cannot imagine, not even for a split second, that this punishment will happen in heaven, because there is no passage of Scripture that mentions punishment when believers are found in heaven.

Remember that this teaching came as a follow-up to Jesus's reply to Peter's question about how many times he was supposed to forgive his brother. This warning from Jesus was directed straight at the disciples, because in the entire chapter of Matthew

18, Jesus is speaking to the disciples. The warning was also directed at each disciple individually. Notice how Jesus mentioned "each of you." The warning remains in effect for every one of us today who professes to be His disciple. The warning is also a call to genuine forgiveness, as Jesus taught that the punishment would be meted out if forgiveness did not proceed from the heart. We must thus pay close attention to ensure that our forgiveness is not just lip service. We cannot fake it. It cannot be superficial. And the ultimate judge is the One who knows the very motives of our hearts. He is saying here that if forgiveness is not from the heart, the consequences will be the same as for the wicked, unforgiving servant.

27 LAST BUT NOT LEAST

A few things have to be said about the aftermath of forgiveness.

1. Forgiveness does not remove the consequences of the offense. Let's look again at Numbers 14. God forgave the people when He said in verse 20, "I have pardoned," yet the consequence of their wrong was still there. They did not enter the promised land (verse 23). So, after you have forgiven the offender, the broken relationship may still be broken, and the lost trust may still be lost. However, you now have peace, love, and compassion toward the offender, and your desire is that they be saved and forgiven.

2. Forgiveness does not undo or repair the damages of the offenses, and some damages may be permanent. We have heard stories of families that forgave someone who murdered one of their loved ones. Forgiveness will not bring their loved one back to life.

3. How do I now relate to the offender after I have forgiven him or her? The answer to this question depends on the level and nature of the relationship and proximity you have with the offender. If there is no prior relationship with the offender, as when one is offended by a total stranger, then there is no relationship to restore either. You forgive them, pray for them, and move on with your life. On the other hand, if there is a prior relationship, such as family or

friendship, then the aftermath of forgiveness entails reconciliation. There are several reasons for this. You will be bumping into each other at most family or friend gatherings. But reconciliation demands willingness on both sides. If the offender is not ready or willing, reconciliation cannot be forced on them. Our Lord Jesus Himself taught about reconciliation in Matthew 5:23–24, saying "[23]Therefore if you bring your gift to the altar, and there remember that your brother has something against you, [24] leave your gift there before the

altar, and go your way. First be reconciled to your brother, and then come and offer your gift." The word "therefore" at the beginning of the sentence of verses 23–24 implies that Jesus is drawing a conclusion from what precedes those two verses. We read in verse 22 that Jesus is warning "whoever" against being angry with, insulting, and calling his brother names, which are typical responses and attitudes of someone who has been offended towards the offender.

4. A few notes of caution: i) even after reconciliation, rebuilding trust takes time; and ii) if the offense consisted of or included abuse and harm, whether physical or emotional, care must be taken not to be exposed to potential harm again. This has nothing to do with the fact that you have forgiven the offender in the first place; it has to do with whether or not the offender has changed their behavior.

5. Don't go back on it! Don't keep repeating the matter. When God forgives, He forgets (Jeremiah 31:34). Not that God loses His memory, but He chooses not to remember. We need to learn to set aside the thoughts that bring back the offenses, choose not to focus on the offenses, and not let our attitude and behavior be conditioned and dominated by the offenses.

Remember that it is God who grants anyone repentance (according to Acts 11:18 and 2 Timothy 2:25) and draws people to Jesus (John 6:44) for salvation. You must therefore pray that God will draw the offender to Jesus, grant them repentance, and deliver them from the real enemy of their soul.

REFERENCES

Brother Lawrence (1989): The practice of the presence of God. Baker books, 1989. ISBN: 0800785991.

Corrie Ten Boom (1971), John and Elizabeth Sherrill: The hiding place. Chosen Books, Grand Rapids, Michigan. ISBN 978-1-59856-339-9.

ABOUT THE AUTHOR

Hans E. Ngodock is a native of Cameroon in Central Africa. He moved to the US after graduate school in France. He is married to his wife Berthe, and together, they are raising four children. Hans has been involved in ministry in various capacities for 30 years. Hans is an ordained minister specializing in youth ministry and discipleship. He loves teaching Bible studies in small groups. In the last 20 years, his passion for foreign missions has led him to many countries (Brazil, Mexico, Sierra Leone, Burkina Faso and India), to train pastors and church leaders.